Navigating Life's Transitions

Real-Life Mindfulness Strategies to Find Purpose, Build Resilience, and Thrive Through Change

By

Steven F. Hick

Copyright © 2025 Steven F. Hick

All rights reserved.

No part of this publication may be reproduced, stored in a retrieval system, or transmitted in any form or by any means—electronic, mechanical, photocopying, recording, or otherwise—without prior written permission from the publisher, except in the case of brief quotations used in reviews or articles.

This book is the product of years of reflection, research, and lived experience. While it is designed to be informative and supportive, it should not be considered a substitute for professional advice. If you are facing a medical, psychological, or personal crisis, please seek the guidance of a qualified professional who can meet you where you are.

For permissions or inquiries, please contact: steven.hick@carleton.ca

Electronic ISBN: 978-1-0693408-3-2
Paperback ISBN: 978-1-0693408-4-9
Hardcover ISBN: 978-1-0693408-5-6

Still River Press

About the Author

Steven Hick, PhD, is a retired professor of social work who now serves as a mindfulness guide and Dharma teacher with True North Insight (TNI). He brings over 45 years of experience in mindfulness, meditation, and Tantra yoga, alongside a lifelong dedication to helping people manage stress, emotional pain, and trauma through mindfulness-based practices. As the founder of the Ottawa Insight Meditation Community, he has led a spiritual meditation group for more than 18 years and has taught Mindfulness-Based Stress Reduction (MBSR) to both aspiring teachers and graduate students across Canada.

His journey began with struggle. Faced with dyslexia, autism, and anxiety, he was once told he wasn't suited for higher education. Defying expectations, he earned five degrees, including a PhD in social work, and published nine books. Drawing from decades of academic, clinical, and personal experience, Steven offers practical wisdom grounded in lived experience. His teaching integrates mindfulness, holistic healing, and deep presence to support others on their path to resilience, joy, and awakening.

A Note of Gratitude

By purchasing this book, you've done more than add another title to your shelf. You've supported both the author and the publisher in bringing meaningful work into the world. Your choice keeps independent voices alive and ensures books like this continue to reach those who need them.

Every page you read is part of a larger conversation—between writer and reader, teacher and student, and among all of us learning how to live with more presence, resilience, and care. Your support makes this possible, and for that, I am deeply grateful.

May this book meet you where you are, and may it walk beside you as you grow

Table of Content

Introduction 1

Chapter 1: Caught Between What Was and What's Next 5

    Life's Big Transitions 7

    The Case for Mindfulness for Life's Transitions 10

    Knowing Your Values and Intentions 14

    Reflection 17

Chapter 2: Mindfulness, Plain and Simple 19

    What Mindfulness Is—And Isn't 20

    How Big Changes Affect the Brain 23

    Practical Mindfulness Tools 25

    Reflection 29

Chapter 3: Taking Mindfulness Off the Cushion 31

    Starting the Day with Mindful Awareness and Intentionality 32

    Integrating Mindfulness into Everyday Activities 34

    Walking Meditation as a Formal Meditation Practice 37

    Mindful Evening Reflections for Closure and Rest 38

    Reflection 41

Chapter 4: Holding On, Letting Go: A Mindful Path Through Grief 43

    The Many Faces of Grief 44

    Mindfulness Techniques for Processing Grief and Emotional Release 45

    Mindful Awareness and Changing Old Patterns 48

    Dancing with Grief 51

    Letting Go of the Thoughts That Hold You 53

    Reflection 56

Chapter 5: Relationships Reimagined 57

Shifting Relationship Roles 58
The Power of the Pause 59
Mindful Communication 62
Cultivating Deeper Connections 63
Reflection 65

Chapter 6: Renewing Identity and Purpose 67

The Identity Puzzle 68
Reframing Identity with Mindfulness 71
Mindful Rediscovery of Passion 71
Developing Your Personal Purpose Statement 76
Shifting to Possibility 80
Reflection 81

Chapter 7: Mindfulness for Health and Aging 83

Mindfulness and Physical Well-Being 84
A Deeper Body Scan Meditation 87
Exercise as Mindful Movement 89
Reflection 94

Chapter 8: Emotionally Resilient Living 95

Emotional Intelligence 96
Understanding Emotional Triggers 98
STOP Method for Managing Strong Emotions 100
Mindful Movement and Processing Emotions 104
Reflection 109

Chapter 9: The Art of Letting Go and Beginning Again 111

Why Change Feels Hard 112
Impermanence: Everything Arises and Passes 113
Mindful Adaptability: Thriving Amidst Uncertainty 114

Accepting the Present Moment 115

Pivoting with Purpose 119

Steadying Through Uncertainty 120

Mindful Decision-Making During Change 121

Reflection 122

Chapter 10: Remembering to Remember: How to Make Mindfulness Stick 123

Remembering to Be Mindful 123

Making Mindfulness a Daily Habit 126

Overcoming Common Roadblocks 128

Meditation Challenges 129

Looking to the Future: Embracing Growth and Wisdom 130

Reflection 135

Conclusion 137

References 141

Introduction

The effects of life's changes can sneak up on us. Everyone experiences a kind of crisis when life feels unsteady, unfamiliar, or unpredictable. A role comes to an end, a child moves out, relationships change, a body starts to ache in unfamiliar ways—and suddenly, life feels uncertain. It isn't always dramatic; sometimes it's the quiet absence of what once gave us purpose, or the unsettling question that lingers at the edges of the day: Who am I now, in the midst of this change?

I felt that question press on me when I gave up whitewater kayaking—the activity that had made me feel most alive. After a few too many head bumps and concussions, I had to let it go. Around the same time, we left our quiet countryside home for the noise and bustle of the city. I hadn't realized how grounding that calm setting had been until it was gone. Suddenly, I was restless, out of place, wondering: What now? Who am I without the river and the quiet country mornings?

Then I discovered a dragon boating club in my neighborhood. I had never tried it before, and to be honest, I thought it might be boring compared with the adrenaline of whitewater. Still, I signed up, as I was looking for a way to pass the time and a distraction from what I was missing.

Fortunately, dragon boating helped lift the fog and restore a sense of direction. Slowly, I began to feel alive again.

Now, fifteen years later, I'm still at it. The shift from whitewater kayaking to dragon boating showed me that life's transitions always carry the possibility of renewal, even though they may be painful at the time. I saw that what feels like an ending can be a new beginning if we're willing to stay present and say yes to what life places in front of us.

This is the essence of mindfulness. It doesn't erase the losses or make transitions easy. But it gives us a way to meet them with curiosity and acceptance. It invites us to loosen our grip on what was and soften into what is, even if it feels unfamiliar at first.

Like so many others I know, I was caught between mourning what had ended and fearing what might never begin. That ache of loss is real. But so is the whisper of relief. Life's significant transitions can strip away old identities, but in their place, they offer space. Possibility. What if these transitions are not about decline, but rediscovery? What if the question isn't "How do I get back to who I was?" but rather "Who might I become now?"

There is nothing inherently diminishing about entering this new chapter. In fact, these years can offer more clarity, freedom, and meaning than any we've known before. We have the wisdom to live without prioritizing others' expectations. We can move forward with conscious intention and live according to what is most important to us.

This guidebook is designed to help you navigate life's significant transitions, complete with the turbulence and uncertainty they entail. You won't find universal fixes or band-aid corrections. Instead, you'll be invited to an approach built on contemplation, awareness, and kindness to oneself.

These pages offer exercises and practices designed for everyday life. They include activities to connect with your values, purpose, and intentions; practical techniques to tune into your body and listen to the messages it's sending; and methods to release complex emotions. You'll also encounter specific practices to enhance emotional intelligence and process difficult emotions, as well as exercises and tools to cultivate self-compassion and forgiveness. Additionally, there are practices to be mindful of and accepting of the present moment, strategies to let go of what no longer serves you, and methods to develop resilience and thrive in the face of uncertainty. Finally, you'll encounter practical pointers to help you establish a mindfulness habit and overcome obstacles to maintaining a consistent mindfulness practice.

This may feel like a lot to take in. You might even be wondering, "Can I really do this? My mind is too busy. My life is too busy." Believe me, I know that feeling. I've had my share of midnight brain-marathons, lying awake with questions looping endlessly: Am I running out of time? Did I take the wrong path? What do I actually want—and do I deserve it?

If you find yourself entangled in emotions of grief, regret, or good old restlessness, listen to this. These are not indicators of having done something wrong.

Everybody encounters these potholes. You may have heard of mindfulness as the practice of sitting in complete stillness and reaching an inner state of calm. That's a fairytale. In reality, mindfulness is about sneaking small doses of awareness and kindness into everyday life. For example, I meditate every morning, but if I miss a day, it's no big deal. No fancy cushions needed, either. I meditate on my couch. I pay attention to posture and maintain an upright back, but I've given up on trying to wiggle into a cross-legged position on a cushion. We'll find a way to keep it practical and manageable, even on days when you'd rather binge-watch shows than be mindful.

My own journey has gone through the highs and lows of life, both personally and professionally. Over the past twenty-five years, I have walked alongside dozens of people—some eager, some hesitant—as they dismantled old beliefs and rebuilt their lives from the inside out.

As a therapist, mindfulness teacher, and fellow practitioner, I draw upon science-backed practices, a deep well of compassion, and stories of real transformation.

I have lived with Zen monks and participated in long, silent retreats. However, if something didn't make sense and resonate with me, I jettisoned it. I have learned from every struggle and triumph, including my own. My promise to you is authenticity and unwavering respect for the uniqueness of your experience.

This book is not a manual of quick fixes. It's a companion—full of reflections, practices, and stories—designed to help you steady yourself through life's big changes. You'll find exercises and practices to calm anxiety, reconnect with what matters most, and bring mindfulness into your everyday life. I won't stand above you as a teacher. I'll sit beside you as a fellow traveler.

Chapter 1:
Caught Between What Was and What's Next

When life's transitions arrive, it feels like being caught between the person you used to be and the person you haven't yet become.

"My whole life is changing under my feet." A friend said this during a walk, and those words have remained with me ever since. They captured the angst, possibility, and introspection so common amidst a significant life transition—the sense that every ending carries the seed of a beginning. I recall thinking that some people get stuck in the mourning, dwelling on their losses and not moving forward, and thus allowing the new beginning to pass them by. I wondered why this happens, and what we might do to avoid it.

Not long after that conversation, I stood in front of my closet on a rainy Sunday afternoon. As I looked for a jacket, something on the floor caught my eye. Tucked behind a pair of boots and an old backpack were my mountain biking shoes. I pulled them out and held them. The soles still had caked dirt wedged into the cleats. The straps were frayed, and the stitching along the sides began to split. I used to wear them almost every weekend, tearing down backcountry trails, dodging roots and rocks, sometimes wiping out, flying over the handlebars, laughing all the way. Riding was my way of shaking off a tough week, remembering that I was alive, and being in the moment.

I perched on the edge of the bed and flipped the shoes back and forth in my hands. I hadn't ridden in ages. Not seriously. Life had gotten noisier and busier. I had replaced dirt trails with deadlines. The shoes were tucked away in the back of the closet like a time capsule—evidence that I used to live differently. I didn't weep. But I sat a minute or two longer and reflected. The shoes reminded me of a piece of myself I'd left behind. Not because of failure. Not even deliberately. Simply because I gradually became someone I didn't even realize I was becoming.

That's how life's transitions can unfold. Sometimes, they arrive suddenly—a job loss, a diagnosis, a move. Other times, they build gradually, and we realize their impact only once we begin to feel unsettled. However they arrive, life's changes often cause us to feel that the person we once were no longer feels like who we are meant to be.

There's grief in this sense of endings. But there is also hope. What if this isn't the end of something, but the start of something new and exciting? How can we prepare for and embrace these changes so that we can meet the natural pain of transition without adding extra suffering? As the saying goes, often attributed to Haruki Murakami and rooted in mindfulness teachings: "Pain is inevitable; suffering is optional."

Life's Big Transitions

Life's major transitions can occur at any stage of life. Adolescents face major changes, but they often predominate in later years, when adults face ongoing changes in who they are and what matters to them. At this life phase, individuals tend to reflect seriously on their lives and re-evaluate decisions made during young adulthood. For instance, an individual may revisit enduring ambitions about their profession or redirect their attention to interpersonal relationships after decades of focusing on occupation and advancement. Another widespread phenomenon involves parents questioning their roles when children leave home, creating inner debates about meaning and fulfillment (Infurna et al., 2020). Re-evaluation may generate interests or values new to an individual, such as a greater interest in community service or the arts.

Retirement itself is a major change, disrupting daily routines and impacting finances. It is often imagined as a state of freedom, yet it can feel disorienting as we lose what is familiar and our identity shifts.

The empty nest or children leaving home is another significant transition. When grown children leave, parents may struggle with feelings of loss or emptiness.

Taking on caregiver duties for a parent, managing doctor visits, or handling finances for an elderly loved one is another transition. It can disrupt routines and create emotional and logistical challenges, especially when combined with other responsibilities at work or home (Infurna et al., 2020).

A new career path, whether chosen or forced, can shake our sense of stability and be a significant transition. Along with new opportunities, it often brings uncertainty, self-doubt, and the challenge of starting over.

Adolescence is a time of identity exploration, where teens begin to question who they are amidst shifting roles, relationships, and societal expectations. This ongoing self-discovery can create significant stress as young people navigate unfamiliar internal and external changes.

Divorce, another major life transition, carries a grief that is both personal and relational—the ending of dreams, routines, and identities intertwined. It can leave us feeling raw and uncertain about the future.

Whether through the death of a loved one, the end of a friendship, or the loss of health, grief is perhaps the most universal transition. It is the human experience of love meeting impermanence.

Health issues are another concern. More frequent doctor visits or physical limitations can raise concerns about independence and even death. These fears are exacerbated by comparing oneself with age peers or examining past health choices.

Relationships also undergo changes. Couples sometimes need to renegotiate their time together after the children move out, while friendships may shift as priorities change. For example, a person might drift away from friends made through school activities but form closer bonds with neighbors or groups that share similar interests.

Emotions around all of these changes vary from person to person, but there's often a mix of anxiety, introspection, and occasional optimism. Despite the challenges, life changes can stir hope and excitement. Many people find renewed energy in pursuing passions that have been put on hold (Infurna et al., 2020).

Growth and Self-Acceptance Amidst Change

One of the gifts that comes with life's transitions is that they push us to rediscover what matters most to us. Change often forces us to pause, look inward, and ask: What do I truly value now? What gives me a sense of purpose? What am I passionate about? This can lead to new discoveries about our deepest aspirations and reveal new adventures and opportunities. With newfound clarity, people often begin to spend their time more intentionally.

Transitions can also invite us to grow in new directions. Many adults take on new challenges, such as learning new technologies to keep pace with younger generations, enrolling in leadership training to stay relevant in their careers, or stepping into volunteer roles that offer both contribution and community engagement. Others find joy in side projects or mentoring, discovering talents they never knew they had. These acts of growth aren't just about skills; they're about reminding ourselves that life can still expand, even as it changes.

A key part of navigating transitions is striking a balance between the feelings of loss and the prospect of growth. Whether we're reshaping our identity, acquiring new skills, or learning to be kinder to ourselves, each step presents an opportunity for meaningful transformation. Aging isn't just about decline; it can be a period filled with clarity, renewal, and the opportunity to embrace who we've always been in the process of becoming.

The Case for Mindfulness for Life's Transitions

Mindfulness means paying attention to what's happening right now on purpose, with an open and accepting attitude. It's more than meditation. It is a set of attitudes to life that shows up in ordinary moments. When we pay attention and are receptive to each moment, our approach to life's transitions changes. We can face life's challenges with wisdom, balance, and clarity. On the other hand, when we are on autopilot and not paying attention, we often become reactive, adding an extra layer of stress to our lives. Mindfulness is about living life as it unfolds rather than going through life in a distracted and reactive way.

Life's transitions can feel overwhelming and cause anxiety. Mindfulness offers a way to navigate these challenges, helping us find our purpose, manage our emotions, and respond thoughtfully rather than react automatically.

Here are the primary ways mindfulness can help us handle life's major transitions. We will examine these in detail throughout this book.

1. **Creates Space Between Reaction and Response**

Life transitions often trigger strong emotions—fear, grief, anger, or uncertainty. Mindfulness helps us pause before reacting, providing a space to notice what's happening inside. This pause allows us to respond with clarity rather than falling back into old, habitual patterns.

2. **Eases Stress and Emotional Overwhelm**

Transitions can feel scary and destabilizing. By bringing attention to the present—through the breath, body, or senses—mindfulness calms the nervous system. Research shows it lowers stress hormones, reduces anxiety, and steadies mood, making it easier to ride out uncertainty without becoming consumed by it.

3. Strengthens Self-Acceptance and Compassion

Big changes often stir self-judgment: "I should be handling this better" or "I'm falling behind." Mindfulness trains us to meet thoughts and feelings without judgment. Over time, this fosters self-acceptance and kindness toward ourselves, which are essential when facing loss, aging, or shifts in identity.

4. Opens the Door to New Perspectives and Possibilities

Transitions can feel like endings, but mindfulness helps us see them as openings, too. By softening our grip on "what was," we create room for curiosity about "what is." This openness allows new values, priorities, and opportunities to emerge, transforming transitions into times of growth and renewal.

Mindfulness: My Companion Through Change

When our children moved across the country, the house felt achingly quiet. At first, the silence was pure loss. But mindfulness helped me sit with the grief instead of fighting it. Over time, that same quiet became space for reflection, creativity, and rediscovering passions I'd set aside.

Retirement was another surprise. I thought I'd feel free, but instead I felt unmoored without my old title and routines. What helped was a simple practice: three mindful breaths with my feet on the floor each morning. That pause reminded me that each day still mattered, and slowly, a new purpose began to take shape.

Moving from the countryside to the city shook me deeply. I missed the stillness of nature and felt restless in all the noise. Mindfulness taught me to stay with that discomfort until I could see what the city offered: community, new rhythms, and, unexpectedly, dragon boating.

Caring for my aging parents brought frustration and guilt. I learned to take one mindful breath before responding. That pause softened my reactions and allowed me to see caregiving not as a burden but as love in action.

Each transition hurt in its own way. But with mindfulness, I could meet the discomfort directly—and discover the openings hidden inside the losses.

Science Meets Daily Life: Mindfulness in Action

Research has shown that people who practice mindfulness report lower stress levels, improved mood, and a greater sense of overall well-being (Bartlett et al., 2021). In everyday life, this can mean drifting off to sleep more quickly after a busy day because you've learned how to soothe a restless mind rather than worrying over every little detail. Instead of staying awake replaying arguments or stressing about tomorrow, you kindly refocus your attention on your breath or the comforting sensation of your body resting on the sheets.

My go-to bedtime practice is to place my hand on my belly and focus my attention on the sensation of my belly rising and falling with each breath. Over time, this simple act reduces nighttime anxiety and leads to deeper, more restful sleep.

Mood also improves because mindfulness trains you to spot early signs of irritation or frustration. Rather than letting negative thoughts snowball, you learn to observe them as they arise. Let's say you face criticism at work. Instead of instantly feeling defeated or angry, you acknowledge the sting and then choose how to respond. You might decide to ask for helpful feedback instead. This ability to stay anchored in the present enhances emotional resilience, making it easier to recover from everyday setbacks (Bartlett et al., 2021; Schuman-Olivier et al., 2020).

Mindfulness provides a crucial pause between what happens and how you react. It's like giving yourself a gentle pause, allowing you to notice your feelings, name them, sense into how they feel in your body, and pause before responding. This brief moment creates an opportunity for you to make thoughtful choices rather than reacting impulsively. It helps you feel less likely to lash out or withdraw, and with time, it builds clarity and confidence to navigate life's twists and turns (Schuman-Olivier et al., 2020).

Mindfulness encourages you to approach each moment with a fresh perspective. This openness allows you to see new possibilities that stress might have hidden. Instead of endless worrying about what could go wrong, you learn to focus on the simple, tangible steps you can take right now.

Mindfulness training reduces perceived stress and even boosts engagement in life. People who practice regularly tend to feel more energetic and have a sense of purpose. They navigate problems with steadier moods and sharper thinking than those caught up in distraction or worry (Bartlett et al., 2021). Mindfulness doesn't erase difficulties, but it helps you handle them with greater balance and clarity.

While these basic mindfulness concepts provide some understanding for dealing with life's difficulties, Chapter 2 will show how science demonstrates that mindfulness can physically change your brain. For now, let's just have fun exploring how you can positively impact your daily experience with these basic principles.

Knowing Your Values and Intentions

When going through significant life changes, whether in adolescence, midlife, or old age, it's essential to know what truly matters and make thoughtful decisions about the future.

Life's turning points invite you to pause and reflect, allowing you to uncover the values that guide you forward. This exercise is about listening inwardly and allowing your truth to emerge on the page.

Step 1: Prepare Your Space

Choose a place where you won't be interrupted. Bring a notebook and a pen. You can use a keyboard, but using the old-fashioned pen tends to make it more grounding. Set a timer for 15 minutes.

Step 2: Freewrite Without Censoring

Begin writing freely—without worrying about grammar, spelling, or whether your words make sense. Let your pen (or keyboard) move as quickly as your thoughts. Trust that whatever comes is exactly what needs to come.

Use these prompts if you need a starting point:

- What does this stage of my life mean to me?

- What do I wish would change?

- What am I proud of from recent years?

- What worries or hopes keep arising?

Even if your words feel scattered, messy, or repetitive, keep writing. You might find yourself admitting, "I feel both excitement and fear about becoming an empty nester," or "I've lost touch with old passions and I want to find them again." If you get stuck, pause and notice your breath, then jot down what you feel in your body or what thoughts are drifting through your mind. No judgment is needed—everything belongs.

Step 3: Gently Review Your Words

When the timer rings, take a breath before re-reading what you've written. Let curiosity guide you rather than self-criticism. Ask yourself:

- What themes or events emerged again and again?

- What feelings stand out most strongly?

- Did anything surprise me?

- Where do I sense longing, resistance, or energy for change?

If emotions feel overwhelming, pause, and remind yourself: This is exploration, not judgment. I am practicing self-discovery, not self-criticism (Miller, 2020).

Step 4: Clarify Your Guiding Values

We can navigate life's transitions more easily when we know what matters most to us. We will go deeper into this in a later chapter with a *Personal Purpose Statement*, but for now, let's examine values. Review what you have written, noticing which values stand out and which ones you feel called to strengthen. For example, if your reflections were about wanting to rekindle joy, perhaps creativity or adventure are values to prioritize. If you wrote about caregiving or parenting, compassion or family might stand at the center.

Set a timer for five minutes and circle the words that feel most important right now. Aim for ten to fifteen. Next, define what each value means to you—what does "growth" or "stability," for instance, look like in your life? Reflect on moments when these values have guided big decisions or brought you comfort.

Next, narrow your list to your top five values, ranking them in order of importance. Notice if some values have shifted in priority. Perhaps "adventure" gains importance as children leave home, or "health" becomes central after a health crisis. Perhaps family has always come first, but lately you're realizing creativity needs more space in your routine.

If ranking feels tough, imagine a week lived fully according to each value to see which one brings the greatest joy or peace. If confusion arises, trust your first instincts and know you can adjust your list over time (Lumia, 2023).

Personal Commitment Statement

Next, take a moment to write a personal commitment statement. This is a short and heartfelt declaration that turns your reflections into clear, focused steps forward. A helpful tip is to follow this simple formula:

"I commit to [specific action], so I can better honor [core value(s)] during this part of my life."

Ensure that you have set achievable goals that reflect your priorities. For example, consider saying: "I commit to exercising three times a week to increase my health and energy," or "I will connect with friends monthly to deepen my social connections," or even "I will dedicate Sunday evenings to playing my trombone."

Take a moment to say your statement aloud, and notice if it feels honest and inspiring. Feel free to tweak the words until they truly resonate with you. Keep your commitment somewhere visible and check in on it regularly (Miller, 2020).

As you work through these exercises, be gentle with yourself and allow for flexibility. There's no one perfect way to set intentions, like there's no single "right" commitment statement or value ranking. These tools are just the beginning and will prepare you for the helpful mindfulness strategies in Chapter 2, where you'll learn how to stay committed even when life gets busy and messy.

Reflection

Looking back at what big transitions mean for many of us, it's basically a mix of "Wait, what now?" and "Maybe this could actually be interesting." It's about being able to stand at a crossroads and remain curious. Each new chapter presents a valuable opportunity to pause, reflect, and identify what truly matters most. Mindfulness won't magically make the confusion disappear, but it does help you face it with a bit more curiosity and a bit less "What did I just do with my life?" panic.

By exploring our values and setting intentions, we create space for new growth. Instead of seeing life's changes only as loss or struggle, we can approach it as a new adventure full of possibilities. In my unfolding life, I had to learn to trust myself—to trust that I could rediscover a life filled with purpose and clarity.

Chapter 2:
Mindfulness, Plain and Simple

I have practiced mindfulness for 45 years and have been teaching it for 20. Currently, I believe that while mindfulness is easy to explain, it can be difficult for many people to actually practice. Numerous myths about mindfulness hinder people's efforts to cultivate it.

Mindfulness helps us reclaim the moments of our lives that pass by unnoticed if we're not attentive. It invites us to notice what's happening without judging it as good or bad. When we fall into judgment, we often respond by resisting or clinging, and that tendency is what leads to our suffering.

In this chapter, I explore how we can engage more fully with everyday life through mindfulness and acceptance. Along the way, I reflect on how our habits and brains adapt during life's major transitions, how this time brings both challenges and new opportunities, and why common beliefs about mindfulness may not align with real-life experiences. I also introduce four foundational and practical tools that fit busy and ever-changing lives.

What Mindfulness Is—And Isn't

Mindfulness means paying attention to what is happening right now without rushing ahead, judging, or trying to change anything. It's about bringing attention to our everyday lives. When you do this, you are not focused on worries, lists, or memories. You are simply noticing what is here. This simple act of noticing, on purpose, is a core part of mindfulness. The other key piece is accepting or not judging what is noticed. This may feel unfamiliar or even sound scary at first, but it's critical, and we'll discuss it more later.

Many people believe that being mindful requires sitting silently for long periods, but in reality, formal meditation is just one way to develop mindfulness. It can also be practiced in regular daily activities, which we will explore in detail in the next chapter. When you pause at a red light and feel the steering wheel in your hands, when you listen carefully as a friend talks about their day, or even when you take a deep breath before opening an important email—these are all chances to practice mindfulness.

Striving Can Hinder Mindfulness

When I first started practicing mindfulness, I thought I was failing. I believed the goal was to sit on the floor for long periods, cross-legged on a cushion, and stop thinking altogether. Being on the autistic spectrum, I clung to this idea with everything I had. I followed the rules. I kept my posture perfect. And the second a thought appeared, I'd scold myself, believing I wasn't trying hard enough.

So, I tried harder. I sat longer. I went to long, silent retreats. But the more I tried to stop my thoughts, the louder they became. The more I strived for perfection, the harder the practice became. It wasn't until later that I began to understand what mindfulness actually is and isn't. Mindfulness isn't about clearing your mind; it's about paying attention to what's already going on. The goal isn't to stop thinking. I realized it's about noticing when I'm thinking, without judging myself. I realized it is about gently bringing my attention back to the present. That might be my breath. It might be my body. It might be the feel of water on my hands as I wash the dishes. Thoughts still come. That's normal. I realized I don't have to chase them.

Mindfulness isn't about control. It's about curiosity and acceptance. It's about learning to be with yourself, even when your mind is noisy. Especially then.

Religion and Spiritual Beliefs

Some people worry that mindfulness conflicts with their religious beliefs or means adopting a new philosophy or spiritual approach. In reality, mindfulness is a practical skill that anyone can use, regardless of their background, faith, or spiritual tradition. It fits easily into any belief system and doesn't require a change in lifestyle. For example, a person managing a chronic illness can use mindful breathing while waiting for medical results. Someone working long hours can take brief, mindful pauses during the day, perhaps by really listening to music on the drive home or by savoring the smell of dinner cooking when they arrive.

Not for Me, It's for Clam People

People often assume mindfulness is for naturally calm people. I used to believe that, too. But I've never been calm by nature. Even as a child, I was anxious. Thankfully, mindfulness has helped me tremendously in dealing with my anxiety and lack of calm. Mindfulness, and particularly body awareness, helped me survive early university studies and employment.

In the mid-1980s, I was in the Philippines working on human rights matters amidst political upheaval. It was important and dangerous work, and stress and fear kept my nervous system revving high. I was short-tempered, tense, and frequently fatigued. When things got really challenging, I started to apply the body awareness practice that I learned in university, and it became my refuge.

When I first learned about mindfulness, I figured it was something meant for other people—those who could be still for hours, whose thoughts didn't run a mile a minute, who hadn't been forged by trauma. But I was mistaken. Mindfulness isn't about being peaceful. It's not about blocking anxiety or compelling peacefulness. It's about being present with whatever is present, whether it's anxiety, tension, or noise, and noticing it without judgment.

People who think they have no extra time for mindfulness often discover that everyday tasks, such as washing dishes, folding laundry, or feeding a pet, can be wonderful moments to practice mindfulness. These simple activities become valuable opportunities to connect and find calm.

Understanding these basic concepts unlocks the door to more advanced skills and practices. As you learn to recognize ordinary moments as opportunities for mindfulness, you begin to build momentum in your mindfulness practice. As you move through the book, you'll see how simple, mindful habits can turn into lasting, supportive practices for your well-being. Whether your goal is to cope better at work, enjoy more meaningful relationships, or prioritize your health, the foundation you establish now with mindfulness makes future growth possible.

How Big Changes Affect the Brain

The brain's ability to change, known as neuroplasticity, stays intact throughout aging. Neuroplasticity is the brain's impressive capacity to reshape itself by forming new neural connections in response to learning and experience (Gazerani, 2025). Imagine someone learning to cook a complex dish or learning to play the drums. Each new skill learned pushes the brain to create new neural pathways. These changes can be observed physically in the brain, where increased activity and development occur in areas associated with the learned activity.

Mindfulness meditation provides an accessible example: studies show that regular practice leads to structural changes in the prefrontal cortex, hippocampus, and other key areas associated with awareness and self-control (Phillips, 2017). When people dedicate themselves to mindfulness, even for just a few weeks, scientists have observed growth in gray matter density in these regions.

Mindfulness practices offer a powerful counterbalance to stress. Through regular mindfulness meditation, people stimulate specific parts of the brain that dampen the body's stress response. This not only lowers cortisol levels but also encourages the growth of new synapses in affected regions, rebuilding what chronic stress has eroded (Phillips, 2017).

For example, when someone spends ten minutes daily focusing on their breath instead of ruminating over anxious thoughts, brain scans show less shrinking in the hippocampus and stronger connections in the prefrontal cortex. These physical shifts bring practical benefits, including reduced forgetfulness, a steadier mood, and greater clarity in day-to-day decision-making.

Later years of life are a time when emotional patterns, built up over decades, tend to repeat more easily. These habitual reactions, such as snapping in frustration or falling into worry, are ingrained in neural circuits through years of repetition.

Practicing mindfulness gently breaks these habitual patterns. When you take a moment to come into the present moment, you open up space to notice your habitual patterns before reacting. Over time, this mindful pause helps forge new neural pathways, making it easier to respond in more positive and healthy ways.

For example, someone who often feels impatient can learn through mindfulness to pause and react calmly instead of automatically snapping. I know this firsthand. When I told my mindfulness teacher how grocery store lines cause impatience in me, he gave me a challenge. He said, for a month, go to the store every day, pick one item, and stand in the longest line. Just watch what happens.

I noticed tight shoulders, a clenched jaw, and thoughts shouting, "This is so annoying!" As I continued, I saw something else. I began to realize that all these body sensations happen when I am impatient. I started to see impatience not as something to fix, but as a series of sensations and thoughts. Eventually, I understood that I could feel the discomfort without being overwhelmed by it.

These transformations do not happen instantly but develop gradually. Over time, specific regions of the brain are strengthened, including the anterior cingulate cortex, insula, and prefrontal cortex. These areas are sensitive to emotional balance and resilience (Phillips, 2017; Gazerani, 2025). Regular practice of mindfulness activates these areas, creating a feedback loop that promotes greater calmness and openness in the face of stressors. Research indicates that regular practice leads to improvements in managing adversity, enabling individuals to recover more quickly from challenges. This enhanced resilience impacts both emotional and physical health: people experience fewer stress-related illnesses and recover more quickly from mental setbacks. Additionally, the practice strengthens the brain's "reserve," improving its capacity to resist decline and recover from injury or illness, which helps protect cognitive and emotional well-being into old age (Phillips, 2017).

By using mindfulness to support neuroplasticity, anyone can cultivate a mind that remains curious, adaptable, and emotionally resilient well into old age (Gazerani, 2025; Phillips, 2017).

Practical Mindfulness Tools

A well-rounded mindfulness routine combines techniques that strengthen attention, increase present-moment awareness, cultivate acceptance and self-compassion, and rewire the brain's response to stress. Four key strategies—breath awareness, body scan, mindfulness bell, and the timer method—form a foundational toolkit for supporting these developments. These four strategies will prepare you for taking mindfulness off the cushion, which we explore in the next chapter.

Understanding Breath Awareness

Breath awareness is simply paying attention to the sensations in your body as you inhale and exhale. It means observing your breath as it goes in and out without trying to control or judge it. You might feel the breath at the nostrils, the belly, or the chest. When you do this, you allow yourself to be present in the moment. The breath becomes your anchor to the present moment. When you feel lost in thought or emotion, the breath becomes your home base, bringing you back to the present moment.

To start breath awareness, find a comfortable place to sit. This might be a chair, a couch, or the floor on a cushion. Sit comfortably, with your back straight but not stiff. Close your eyes if it feels good, or keep them soft and open, gazing at the floor in front of you. Then, bring your attention to your breath. Feel the air moving in and out of your nostrils. You can also notice your chest or belly rising and falling with each breath.

When first starting with this practice, an effective way to keep your focus is to count each breath. When you breathe in, say "one" in your mind, then when you breathe out, say "two." Keep counting up to ten and then start again at one. If you find your mind wandering and thinking about other things, that's okay. Gently bring your attention back to your breathing and start counting from one again. This helps train your mind to return to the present moment.

When you focus gently on your breath, it triggers a natural response in your body called the relaxation response. This means your nervous system shifts from a state of stress to calmness. Stress usually causes your heart to beat faster and your muscles to tense up. By paying attention to your breathing, your heart rate slows, and your muscles relax.

Focusing attention on the breath trains the mind to stay with one thing at a time. It's a practice of gathering scattered attention and settling it. At first, it may feel impossible. The mind jumps from one thought to the next. But with patience, something shifts. The breath becomes not just a point of focus, but a place of steadiness, an anchor to the present moment.

If you are interested in guided meditation to get started, consider my "10-Minute Mindfulness Meditation," available on Insight Timer, a platform that combines both an app and a website. Simply search for "10 Minutes Mindfulness Meditation" by Steven Hick.

Body Scan Practice

I will briefly introduce the body scan, but it is a core practice, and I will go into further detail later. The body scan involves bringing gentle, curious attention to different parts of your body, one area at a time. You might begin at the crown of your head and slowly move down through your face, neck, shoulders, arms, chest, abdomen, hips, legs, and finally your feet. The goal isn't to fix or change anything, but simply to notice what sensations are present. Is there tingling? Warmth? Tension? Maybe even numbness? All sensations are welcome, even the absence of sensation. By practicing openness and acceptance, you create a safe internal space where your body's messages can be heard rather than ignored or judged.

The benefits of a regular body scan go far beyond momentary relaxation. Over time, it sharpens your ability to detect the subtle shifts in your body that often signal deeper emotional or physical states. You might begin to notice that your jaw clenches when you feel anxious, or your stomach knots during certain conversations. These early warning signs are often missed in the rush of daily life, but mindfulness helps you catch them sooner. And with that awareness comes choice. You can stretch, breathe, or take a mindful pause before tension turns into a headache or a sharp word slips out in frustration.

Body scans also foster a sense of wholeness and connection. Many of us live in our heads, treating our bodies like vehicles to carry us from one task to the next. But when you tune in regularly, the body becomes less of an afterthought and more of a guide. It anchors you in the present moment, softens your reactivity, and gently reminds you that you are not just a thinking mind. You are a sensing, feeling human being. We'll go deeper into the "how-to" of the body scan in Chapter 7, but for now, know this: it's not about perfect attention. It's about showing up, moment by moment, and letting your body teach you what presence really feels like.

Mindfulness Bell

The timer method provides a structured approach to cultivating consistency in mindfulness. The bell signals us to practice a short mindfulness session. Over time, this turns mindfulness into a habit.

To practice, set a bell to chime at the same time each day, such as lunchtime or just before bed, or at random. When the bell sounds, stop and bring your full attention to breath awareness or body scanning. Consistent use of this method will rewire neural circuits to support consistency. Here, we are making formal mindfulness practice a habit. You can use the Mindfulness Bell app and select "random" under the "ring every" heading.

Meditation Timer

I recommend using a timer for your meditations. I use the Insight Timer app, which offers thousands of guided meditations. I have about 40 meditations stored there. Using a timer for meditation creates a transparent container for your practice, allowing you to fully settle in without the mental chatter of "How long has it been?" or the temptation to keep checking the clock. It signals a beginning and an end, which helps build trust in the routine and makes it easier to commit, even if it's just five or ten minutes. Knowing that the timer will alert you when it's time to stop gives your mind permission to let go and be fully present. Over time, this simple tool supports consistency, reduces resistance, and reinforces the idea that you're making space for something valuable: your own well-being.

Together, these four practices nurture focused attention, self-awareness, and adaptive response patterns. Mastery of breath awareness enhances the brain's relaxation pathways, body scanning builds early detection skills for stress, and the bell and timer methods ensure regular practice. Equipped with these skills, daily challenges become opportunities for mindful engagement instead of sources of reactivity. Because these methods address both mind and body, they create a solid foundation for deepening resilience and thriving in the face of change. Practicing these tools regularly sets the stage for applying more advanced techniques later, such as cultivating compassion or using mindfulness to address complex emotional challenges, which are covered in subsequent chapters.

Reflection

As I reflect on these ideas, I realize how much of my own daily experience is shaped by what I pay attention to. If my mind is scattered, I am more likely to react and be stressed. If my mind is focused on what is happening in each moment, I feel more capable of responding to challenges.

Mindfulness is not only about long, silent meditations. By practicing short, focused techniques such as breath awareness, body scanning, and using a bell and timer, I've found that there are small ways to interrupt stress and invite a sense of calm, even in hectic periods. These approaches don't require dramatic shifts or significant additional time—just moments of honest attention to what's happening right now. The more I practice mindfulness, the easier it becomes to recognize my patterns and pay attention to my life as it unfolds. As I look forward, I see that these simple practices are about shaping a mind that remains flexible, present, and open to growth, regardless of where I am in life or what significant transitions I face.

Chapter 3:
Taking Mindfulness Off the Cushion

I used to think that mindfulness was all about calming the mind and sitting quietly for long stretches. I didn't realize the bigger picture until a teacher explained, "We don't meditate to become great meditators; we meditate so we're more likely to be mindful throughout our day." She likened it to tuning an instrument before taking the stage. Remember, the meditation cushion isn't the main event—it's just the preparation for what's to come.

That one comment changed how I approached mindfulness. I began to see it not as a practice confined to formal settings, but as something that could weave through the entire day, in how I got out of bed, made my tea, and walked down the stairs. These weren't distractions from mindfulness. They were the moments it was meant for.

This chapter is about those ordinary moments—the in-between spaces where life actually happens. We'll explore what it means to wake up not just *in* the morning, but *to* the morning, and how to bring attention and intention to even the smallest daily activities. You don't need more time, just a little more presence. Together, we'll explore small activities that focus attention on the present, plant seeds of intention, and reflect at night to end with awareness. Each part encourages noticing what's quietly present amid busyness.

Starting the Day with Mindful Awareness and Intentionality

Rushing through the early moments of the day, scrolling through messages, jumping out of bed, and immediately shifting into "doing" mode often leaves people feeling stressed and unsettled. The simplest gateway into morning mindfulness starts before even getting out of bed. When we start the day with mindfulness, it lays the foundation for more mindful moments throughout the day.

Morning Mindfulness

Try noticing your body, breath, and the sounds in the room before you jump out of bed. Notice the sensation of your body against the mattress, the gentle pressure of your head on the pillow, and the way each muscle softens or tenses. Paying attention to these sensations is mindfulness itself—it lays the foundation for greater awareness throughout the day. If discomfort or tension is present, acknowledge it too, without judgment.

After rising, continue this sense of gentle observation with a short breathing practice. I do a quick meditation each morning before I grab my coffee or do anything else. I get up out of bed and sit or lie down on the couch. I set a timer for two minutes, close my eyes, and notice the natural rhythm of my breath as it enters and leaves my body. I don't try to change the breath. I simply watch its flow. When my mind wanders, which it usually does, I kindly guide it back to the next inhalation or exhalation.

Distraction is normal. Each return to the breath is, in itself, an act of mindfulness. When the timer sounds, I pause and take note of how I feel. For me, practicing for just two or three minutes in the morning can set the tone for the rest of the day.

After my mini-meditation, I think about how I would like to move into the day. Making daily intentions is like sowing a seed for the sort of day you'd like to cultivate. You might set intentions such as patience, curiosity, or compassion. Take a moment to consider what these intentions would look like in your daily life. Is there a quality you'd like to develop, or a challenge you anticipate facing? Whisper your word or phrase to yourself and take it with you throughout the day.

To further strengthen awareness, start with a simple reflection: "This morning, I noticed..." Write the prompt at the top of a page, then jot down whatever comes to mind. Perhaps you've noticed feelings of tiredness, hunger, anxiety, or joy. Let the words flow freely without judging them. This exercise in reflective noticing keeps you grounded in the present and helps you meet yourself where you are. Even on busy mornings, a single sentence can shift your focus from autopilot to conscious living (Fiese et al., 2002; Nell Derick Debevoise, 2024).

Each of these steps—mindful breathing, intention-setting, and reflective noticing—lays the groundwork for bringing presence into your life. It is all about returning again and again to the habits of noticing and allowing, recognizing that growth happens gradually (Arlinghaus & Johnston, 2018; Lally et al., 2010).

If mornings are rushed or filled with responsibilities, adapt these practices as needed. Perhaps your morning mini-meditation is as simple as taking three deep breaths before getting out of bed, or setting an intention while brushing your teeth.

Integrating Mindfulness into Everyday Activities

Throughout the day, many people find themselves moving from one task to another on autopilot. This happens because routines become so familiar that we stop paying conscious attention, allowing our minds to wander to worries about the future or replay memories of the past. As a result, valuable time slips away without being truly experienced (Wein, 2021). The good news is that these everyday moments are perfect opportunities to bring mindfulness off the cushion and into real life, expanding presence beyond formal meditation.

Mindful Walking

Mindful walking is a core practice and one of my favorites. It can be an informal practice where you simply notice the sensation in your body in motion, whether heading to work, strolling through a park, or just moving around in your home. To practice mindful walking, start by feeling the connection between your feet and the ground. As you take a step, focus on the sensation of your heel hitting the floor and how your weight shifts from one leg to the other. Notice the subtle movement of your arms and changes in balance as you walk. Try to anchor your attention in these bodily sensations, gently bringing it back whenever your mind drifts to thoughts.

Common challenges include feeling self-conscious or distracted by surroundings. If this happens, try walking a bit slower at first. It may be helpful to practice mindful walking indoors or in a quiet space before taking it outside. Over time, you will notice it becomes easier to return to the present moment, even in busy environments.

One small shift that worked surprisingly well for me was choosing to walk the dog mindfully. I made a commitment to walk mindfully whenever I take the dog for a walk. If I noticed I was halfway around the block and lost in thought, I'd gently bring my attention back to walking. It was a way to gently say to myself, "Let's try that again, with presence this time."

While mindful walking is a core practice, mindfulness can be brought into any activity. It could be as simple as brushing your teeth, washing a dish, folding laundry, or taking a step outside. Whatever you choose to do, make a point of doing it like you care. You may feel the rhythm of your movement, bring awareness to the pressure on your feet, sense the texture of what you are touching, or feel the temperature of the air.

All of this requires only that you allow yourself to fully be in it—even for just a few breaths. And if your mind wanders, which it will, bring it back gently. No judgment. No expectation to "get it right." Just come back to the practice. I want to stress that *coming back* to your experience is the essential muscle you build in your practice. The more you do small things that require you to return, the more that awareness will become stitched into the everyday fabric of your life. And remember, it also changes your brain.

Mindful Eating

Mindful eating provides a similarly rich option for practicing mindfulness. Choose just one meal today to fully experience. Start by examining your food, noticing the colors, arrangement, and any smells. When you take a piece of food into your mouth, pay attention to the texture and the temperature. After you chew your food, take note of the changes in flavor, the consistency, and the physical sensation of swallowing. Pause occasionally to check in with your hunger and fullness cues, or simply to appreciate any food still in front of you (Wein, 2021).

It can be tempting to reach for your phone or turn on the TV during meals, but try to eat in silence for just a few minutes. If your mind wanders, redirect your attention back to the meal. With each meal, you may discover unique flavors or new sensations of satisfaction. You may notice over time that there are longer stretches of focused attention, decreased mindless snacking, and more enjoyment of eating.

Environmental Cues

Present-moment reminders, also known as environmental cues, can help you stay mindful throughout the day. Pick common objects that you encounter often, such as doorframes, red traffic lights, or the sound of a notification. There is an app called Mindfulness Bell that can also be used. It is a bell you set to ring randomly or at specified intervals. I used to place notes around the house that said, "Now." Whenever you see or hear your chosen cue, use it as a prompt to pause, breathe, and check in with yourself: What am I feeling right now? Where is my attention? (Wein, 2021).

Sometimes, these reminders are easy to overlook when you're rushing or stressed. It helps to start with just one cue while building the habit. For instance, every time you hold a doorknob, take a slow breath and, within that breath, anchor your awareness on the sensation of the doorknob. Once you are comfortable, you can gradually switch to multiple cues. Over time, being present more often without making a conscious choice reflects the true integration of attention and mindfulness into daily living.

The difficulty with mindfulness activities is that it's easy to slip back into autopilot or rush to finish chores quickly. Practicing patience and curiosity with ordinary experiences can make them feel more rewarding. Over time, you'll recognize a growing ability to be present during any activity, not just special ones.

Carrying mindfulness from morning routines into these everyday moments is a key part of the mindfulness journey. Remember, the goal is gentle, consistent effort—returning, again and again, to what is happening right now. Each small instance of awareness makes a difference. These practices naturally build a foundation for emotional awareness by making it easier to observe shifting moods and feelings. Becoming more present with daily activities prepares you to explore deeper emotional states with additional practices, which the next chapters will explore further.

Walking Meditation as a Formal Meditation Practice

I'd practiced mindful walking for years, but it wasn't until a retreat with Thich Nhat Hanh that I truly felt its weight. The retreat hosted over 3,500 people, with meditations held in a football stadium. I happened to be staying in the farthest residence, next door to Thich Nhat Hanh himself. Each morning began with a slow, silent walk to the stadium. We moved together, step by step, collecting more participants as we went. By the time we arrived—forty-five minutes later—thousands of us entered in shared silence. That quiet energy, carried on the rhythm of feet and breath, was unlike anything I'd experienced. A walking community, bound not by words but by presence.

Major life transitions often accelerate the pace of life, with faster decision-making, shifting roles, and increased responsibility. Mindful walking does the opposite. It invites us to slow down and return to something simple, the feeling of our feet on the ground. Each step becomes a way to reconnect with the present moment.

You don't need a meditation retreat to do this. Any place will do, such as a hallway, a backyard, or the edge of a park. I have introduced informal mindful walking, but the practice can be done as a kind of formal meditation. To do this, pick a set path so you don't have to think about where you are going. I usually pick a 15-foot path. Some people prefer to do it barefoot on the grass. Start at one end of the path by standing still, then begin walking very slowly, paying attention to how your body moves. Focus attention on the sensations in your feet to start. When your mind wanders, gently return to the feeling of your steps. No need to force anything. The rhythm will hold you. The ground will meet you.

Mindful Evening Reflections for Closure and Rest

Evening mindfulness practices provide an opportunity to reflect, prepare for sleep, and integrate the day's experiences. It's about taking a moment to acknowledge what has occurred, let go of lingering stress, and soothe the mind and body for a restful sleep (Wright, 2023).

Daily Review and Reflection

A simple exercise is the daily review. It involves identifying a moment when you were fully present. Before bed, ask yourself: What was a moment of presence? You might recall the sight of sunlight filtering through the trees, the song of a bird, or a kind word from a friend. Bringing to mind these smallest moments, which are actually huge, can become anchors of appreciation, helping refocus attention on positivity before sleep.

While the daily review evokes feelings of gratitude, the exercise of naming feelings takes it one step further. In this exercise, you want simply to name and recognize the most substantial feelings from your day. Begin by reviewing your day and asking, "What feelings showed up more prominently and clearly in my day?" Look for more specific feelings, moving beyond general terms like "happy" and "sad," and instead consider how particular words like "relieved," "anxious," "content," "disappointed," or "curious" might work better for you.

Naming Emotions and Letting Go

Naming your feelings can help you assess your emotional state, deepen your emotional literacy, and may even serve as a foundation for recognizing and responding to your needs (Wright, 2023). Name whatever comes up as it arises, without suppressing or engaging in negative self-talk, and remind yourself that all emotions are both valid and transient.

If you are unsure of your feelings, begin by acknowledging your physical sensations. Is your chest tight? Are your shoulders relaxed? Extending these bodily sensations into the names of feelings can help build insight, all of which is possible with just a few sentences on emotional naming and acceptance each night.

The final core practice is letting go, which is intended to release worries and enable genuine rest to occur. Grab a piece of paper or a notebook and write down anything that is causing stress, anxiety, or worry. As the start of the journal entry prompt, you can use: "Tonight I release..." Then complete the sentence. Be honest, say it like you mean it. You can express any fears, anxieties, disappointments, or frustrations you experienced that day.

Once you've written it down, close your eyes and imagine that each concern or worry is a cloud drifting across the sky, or a leaf flowing down a stream. The imagination is a powerful tool that can help you not only release the existing mental clutter but also allow your mind to create space for calmness and rest. If you find that some worries continue to surface, you can remind yourself that this is a nightly practice. The goal is not to eliminate anxiety, but to create more space and lightness, thereby increasing the likelihood of sleep (Wright, 2023).

Spending approximately ten minutes on the overall evening ritual can be an effective use of time, dedicating a few minutes each to review, acknowledge feelings, and let go. If you are busy in the evening, simply selecting one practice is sufficient. The priority is to engage in it regularly, rather than aiming to do everything.

Some examples might show how these practices work in real life. After a long, tiring day at work and struggling to relax, you may use the daily review to reflect on a small act of kindness from a colleague. This can help you focus on gratitude instead of frustration. You might have identified different emotions and, upon reflection, realized that the underlying irritation was actually caused by feelings of sadness and stress. This awareness can open the door to self-compassion.

The letting-go exercise can help you release repetitive thoughts about the next day by starting with a prompt, "Tonight I release...", and visualizing those thoughts floating away.

Adapt these methods to suit your needs: write long entries or short notes, or use voice recordings if writing feels like too much. Consistency is key! Over the course of multiple weeks, these rituals create a strong sense of closure, peace, and readiness not just to sleep comfortably at night but also to approach the upcoming day with slightly more clarity and emotional balance (Nortje, 2020; Wright, 2023).

Reflection

Mindfulness is a powerful way to live. I have noticed that when I am not present with my moment-to-moment experience, life simply slips by. Simple acts, such as being aware in the morning, paying attention through ordinary routines, and reflecting at night, help me step out of automatic patterns.

Even when I rush through life or when emotions become intense, pausing to observe what's really happening can bring clarity and create more space inside. No matter how busy I am, these moments remind me that presence is always within reach, even during the most ordinary times.

As my practice deepens, I notice that I feel less caught up in stress and can truly enjoy each moment as it unfolds. I've realized that if I forget to be mindful, it's no big deal—I can always start fresh and begin again. Every time I become aware, I'm strengthening my mindfulness habit. Reflecting at night helps me let go of what I can't change and opens up space for rest. By incorporating these practices into my daily life, I can care for myself with patience and honesty. Over time, this approach has enabled me to greet each day—and myself—with even greater kindness and curiosity.

Chapter 4:
Holding On, Letting Go: A Mindful Path Through Grief

For fourteen years, our family had a standard poodle named Rambo. He was a loyal and intelligent dog that could sense moods and cheer you up when you were feeling down. When he died, he was missed. I kept catching myself looking for him by the front door, or in his spot in the kitchen under the island where he'd watch the family come and go.

Loss works that way. It can be the death of someone we love, the end of a chapter, or the fading of an old identity. It asks us to surrender what was and learn how to live with what is. Mindfulness doesn't erase the pain. It gives us a way to be with it—softly, steadily—so that love can be felt without being swallowed by it.

Grief has many shapes. Sometimes it's loud and sudden; other times it lingers like a low tide. There's no right way to do this. What helps is honest attention: noticing the weight in the chest, naming the feeling that rises, and offering ourselves a little kindness right where we are. This chapter is about that kind of attention—how to meet loss without hardening, and how to let go without abandoning what mattered.

The Many Faces of Grief

During the early years of adolescence and later in life, especially during retirement or family transitions, your self-concept may undergo significant changes. As you move away from roles such as leader, provider, parent, or expert, you may face self-doubt. Former executives may wonder where they fit now that they no longer have meetings or teams. Parents with empty nests may long for the days when they were busy. Life's routines around daily activities change, prompting re-evaluation of what is meaningful (Lang et al., 2022). Adolescence may shift from identifying as a family member to identifying themselves in multiple ways outside of their role in the family. These shifting roles can cause anxiety, loss, and uncertainty.

Each of these losses can trigger grief. The body and mind respond with a range of emotions, including numbness, yearning, irritability, and sometimes relief or acceptance. Sometimes grief manifests as fatigue or distractibility; other times, it hits with sharp clarity. For some, grief stays as a quiet background; for others, it comes in waves—sudden and unexpected. There are many ways to grieve, and none is more "correct" than another. You might notice changes in your energy, sleep, appetite, or relationships—each is a natural part of navigating change (Lang et al., 2022; Reid, 2022). Recognizing these reactions as normal can reduce shame and foster self-compassion.

Grief can coexist with gratitude or hopefulness. Feeling regret for paths not taken does not erase pride in your choices. Missing the company of a partner or children doesn't mean you're failing at independence. It is just an indicator of how deep the relationship is. Emotions such as anger or sadness flag the extent to which you cared, and by honoring them, you can uncover pathways forward.

As discussed in Chapter 3, mindfulness exercises help us remain present and grounded, particularly when navigating the complex emotions associated with grief and loss. Mindful attention to daily activities and the reflective journaling exercises we practiced provide ways to support ourselves as we navigate grief. Now that we have a basic foundation in mindfulness and an understanding of the causes and results of loss and grief, we can move into strategies for processing grief and releasing what no longer serves us.

Mindfulness Techniques for Processing Grief and Emotional Release

Mindfulness provides an anchor when we experience grief, enabling us to notice and accept our feelings without getting lost in them (Segal, Williams, & Teasdale, 2013; Huang et al., 2020). By focusing on the present with curiosity and compassion, mindfulness can ease overwhelming grief and aid in processing loss (Huang et al., 2019; Roemer, Williston, & Rollins, 2015).

Setting a Space and Time

The initial step in the grieving process is to select a physical space where you can practice. It can be anywhere, really. The emphasis in this stage is to focus on returning to this area at regular intervals each day, even if just for a few minutes, to teach your mind and body that you are entering a safe area where all emotions are welcome and not judged. Committing to returning each day at the same time creates a habit that reinforces this safe space, making it less daunting to approach the difficult feelings as they present in subsequent stages of grieving (Segal et al., 2013).

Feeling in the Body Where Grief Resides

Body-based awareness helps connect the mind and body, revealing how grief is experienced physically. This practice grounds attention in sensations like heaviness, tightness, or warmth. The body scan is especially helpful for this. You may begin to recognize previously unnoticed patterns, such as clenching your jaw before tears appear. If a wave of sensation feels too intense, gently return your awareness to your breath or open your eyes to orient yourself.

For example, we may experience grief when a grown child moves out. When you are packing up their room, you feel a sense of emptiness in your chest, and you realize you need to pause and acknowledge this pain. With mindfulness, instead of pushing it away, we lean into it, trusting it will come and go if we acknowledge it.

Naming Emotions Without Identification

Naming emotions brings clarity and reduces distress by allowing feelings to be seen for what they are. Begin this exercise by sitting quietly and asking yourself: What am I feeling right now? Without analyzing or judging, label whatever arises: sadness, anger, numbness, or relief. To ground this exercise, say the word aloud or write it in a journal. Spend one to two minutes with each named emotion, repeating the label with a gentle attitude. If your mind resists, remind yourself that naming does not mean dwelling; it's simply acknowledging (Bishop, 2004; Segal et al., 2013).

When you name the emotion, try wording it in a different way. Instead of "I am sad," try saying, "Sadness is here." This helps reinforce the idea that sadness does not define you. It lessens any personal identification with the emotion. Instead, you realize it is a temporary visitor. For example, if retiring stirs both excitement and fear, you might notice butterflies in your stomach and say, "Fear is here."

If a flood of emotion threatens to overwhelm you, shift back to observing simple physical sensations or focus on breathing until calm returns (Hölzel et al., 2011; Huang et al., 2019).

Compassionate Breathing

Compassionate breathing is one of the primary strategies for regulating intense emotional currents. Its purpose is to comfort and hold you as emotions flow through. Let's give it a try...

When you are ready, breathe in for a count of four. Do your best to envision calm air filling your lungs. Hold for a beat. Then, breathe out through your mouth for six counts; as you exhale, think about letting go of the tension. Repeat this pattern for three to five minutes. By doing this consistently, you may lower the physical symptoms of anxiety, steady your heart rate, and allow space for the grief to be processed (Goldin & Gross, 2010; Hölzel et al., 2011).

Compassionate breathing is especially useful in moments of transition or loneliness. For example, picture adjusting to a quieter house after retirement. As loneliness creeps in, practicing compassionate breathing offers a gentle reset. By prolonging your exhalation, you signal safety to your nervous system instead of spiraling into worry about the future. This will make it easier to rest in the present moment. Gradually, deeper breaths should come more naturally, and you should feel less overall agitation. If an emotional surge becomes too intense, pause the breathing exercise, stand, stretch, or step outside for a minute before resuming.

These practices encourage a gradual and compassionate release of grief. Mindfulness enables you to proceed at your own pace, building courage by gradually confronting small pieces of pain (Huang et al., 2020). The techniques developed here—namely, body awareness, emotional labeling, and compassionate breathing—will serve as the foundation for resilience and prepare you for the next phase of your mindfulness practice. As you grow more comfortable experiencing difficult emotions safely, you'll be ready to release old patterns and discover new freedoms in the following sections.

Mindful Awareness and Changing Old Patterns

Mindful awareness opens the door to change. The same presence that once sat with grief or pain can now shine a light on the habits that quietly shape our lives. Some of these patterns support us, while others keep us stuck or drain our energy. When we pause long enough to see clearly, we can begin to make different choices. The following five-step process can help us transform old, unhelpful habits into new behaviors that align with our most deeply held aspirations.

Step 1: Ask Three Direct Questions

When you notice yourself repeating an old behavior, pause and ask:

1. Does this behavior reflect who I want to be right now?

2. Am I acting from love or from fear?

3. What cost do I pay by holding onto this habit?

Write these questions on a notecard and place it somewhere you'll see every day—on your bathroom mirror, next to your bed, or taped to your laptop. Each time an automatic pattern arises, use these questions as a compass.

For example, imagine catching yourself cleaning up after your adult children, even though you'd prefer they take responsibility. In that moment, pause and ask: "Does this align with the values I want to live by?" By reflecting honestly, you create space to act from a place of awareness instead of habit.

Step 2: Name What You Feel, Without Judgment

When a limiting pattern comes into view, start by simply acknowledging what's happening inside you. You might say:

- "I feel anxious when things aren't perfect."
- "I feel guilty when I say no."
- "I feel invisible when I don't get recognition."

Notice the emotion. Let it be there. Mindfulness is not about pushing feelings away but about allowing them to be seen and held gently.

Step 3: Shift Your Inner Voice with Compassion

Next, replace harsh or critical thoughts with kinder, more accurate words. This is not about sugar-coating reality—it's about speaking to yourself with the same care you'd give a dear friend.

- Instead of: "I never get this right."
- Try: "I am learning new ways to care for myself."
- Instead of: "I have to say yes or I'll let them down."
- Try: "My needs are valid, too, and saying no can be an act of love."
- Instead of: "I'm too weak to change."
- Try: "I trust myself to grow, one step at a time."

You can also use simple affirmations that plant seeds of kindness:

- "I deserve to be kind to myself."

- "I can rely on myself to make good choices."

- "I am worthy of rest, care, and love."

Step 4: Practice Daily Repetition

Read your affirmations out loud each morning. The sound of your own voice speaking encouragement can shift how you begin the day, softening self-criticism and opening space for growth. If you struggle to find the right words, imagine what you'd say to a close friend going through the same thing—and then offer those same words to yourself.

Step 5: Trust the Slow Transformation

Over time, this practice creates subtle but profound change. Each pause, each kind phrase, begins to rewire your brain and how you relate to yourself. Instead of being pushed around by old habits, you develop the inner strength to act with clarity and compassion.

Letting Go Rituals

Visualization provides reality checks for change. One straightforward way is to use paper and pen. Write the old habit or belief you want to let go of on a little piece of paper and fold it up into your hands. Out loud, say, "Thank you for looking after me. I now release you." Burn the paper in a safe way, noticing how the smoke rises and floats away, while saying goodbye to your old story. Sense into every part of letting go.

Another option is to use water. Find a river or stream and stand on its banks. Pick up a leaf and say your limiting pattern out loud while holding the leaf. Throw the leaf into the flowing water and watch as it moves downstream with the current. As you acknowledge letting go, feel the cool air on your face and breathe in the smell of fresh water.

You can also collect a few small tokens that represent the pattern, such as dried leaves, a piece of string, or an old photo. Put the tokens into a bowl. Add soil, and plant a flower or herb seed. Your plant will grow as you remind yourself that you are also making space for something new.

Release does not always happen on the first try. Approach the process with patience and a curious mindset. Some patterns slip away quickly, while others require repeated effort and support from friends or a trusted coach. Celebrate small shifts (Abu Rayhan, 2023; gabzye, 2023).

As valuable as these rituals of release are, grief also asks to be felt and expressed through the body. Old patterns don't live only in thoughts or symbols—they linger in the breath, in the shoulders, in the heaviness we carry each day. That's why embodied practices are equally important. Movement and rhythm can help release what rituals, words, and reflections cannot. One of the most powerful ways to do this is through dance.

Dancing with Grief

I have found that in my life, grief can be processed through movement and dance. Dance/movement therapy acknowledges how grief manifests in the body—as tension in the chest, heaviness in the limbs, or constriction in the breath. This approach invites us to move rather than suppress, fostering awareness, expression, release, and integration. In the fluidity of movement, grief is neither denied nor exaggerated—it is simply held. Letting our bodies sway, contract, or stretch becomes an act of witnessing the sorrow within, allowing energy that has been trapped to soften and move.

There is also a profound tenderness in turning grief into a dance of survival. Grief and healing are like dance partners—sometimes grief leads, and healing follows; sometimes healing steps forward, and grief retreats. In time, both find their rhythm. Letting go into movement, especially when it is unchoreographed, can offer a state of flow: a movement meditation where the mind quiets and the body whispers its own stories of healing. In dance, sorrow does not just surface—it transforms.

The Elm Dance

One example of this is environmental activist Joanna Macy's Elm Dance. It is a practice that emerged in response to ecological grief and human suffering in areas poisoned by the Chernobyl nuclear disaster. It is done in a circle, which becomes a container of support, reminding each person that grief is not carried alone. The simplicity of the dance allows space for emotion to rise and flow through the body, while the shared ritual (or the imagined community) offers belonging and strength.

Numerous videos of the Elm Dance are available online. Try searching for "The Elm Dance: The Work That Reconnects." To do the elm dance, begin by standing in a circle together. If you are practicing alone, imagine yourself surrounded by others. Now, reach out and take the hands of those beside you—or, if you are alone, gently rest your hands together in front of your chest, as if holding the invisible hands of a wider community. Allow your shoulders to soften, your chest to open, and your gaze to be steady but gentle.

We'll start with a simple sway. Let your body rock from side to side, shifting your weight from one foot to the other. Feel the rhythm in your breath and in your bones. This is the rhythm of life itself—steady, grounding, enduring.

When you are ready, let the sway turn into small steps, moving with the circle, slowly, deliberately. With each step, imagine your roots deepening into the earth, steady and supportive. As the group continues moving together, gently raise your arms upward, as though you are branches reaching for the sky. Stretch into the openness above you. Feel the dignity of the tree, standing strong through all seasons.

Now, let your arms fall again, bowing low, honoring the roots, honoring the ground, honoring the sorrow and love we carry within us. Together we rise and fall, like trees swaying in the wind—sometimes lifted, sometimes bent, always connected.

Let the dance continue in this simple rhythm: swaying, stepping, lifting, bowing. No need to force anything. If tears come, let them. If laughter comes, welcome it, too. Allow your body to express what your heart holds.

As we come to a close, let the movement grow smaller. Return to stillness, feet planted firmly, hands again connected or held close to your heart. Take a breath and notice: Grief is still here, but so is life. You are not alone. The circle holds you.

While movement helps grief find release through the body, grief also lives in the stories we tell ourselves. Thoughts can be just as heavy as physical sensations, shaping how we experience loss. To move forward, it helps not only to free the body but also to gently question the beliefs that keep us stuck. That's where mindful inquiry into thoughts becomes essential.

Letting Go of the Thoughts That Hold You

When grief rises, it often comes not only in waves of feeling but also in the stories we tell ourselves. These stories can feel solid, unshakable—"I'll never be okay again," "I should have done more," or "Without them, I am nothing." Left unquestioned, these thoughts can intensify our suffering, adding layers of fear, regret, or guilt to the rawness of loss. Mindfulness teaches us to notice these thoughts without becoming them, and Byron Katie's practice, known as *The*

Work, offers a simple yet profound way to gently question the truth of these beliefs.

The next time you notice a painful thought surfacing—whether about loss, regret, aging, or identity—pause. Take a breath. Write the thought down if you can, and then bring it to inquiry with these four questions (Katie & Mitchell, 2002):

1. Is it true?

Begin here. Ask yourself honestly: Is this thought actually true? Don't rush. Allow yourself to sit with the question. Sometimes the answer is yes, sometimes no—but even pausing to ask creates space.

2. Can I absolutely know it's true?

This question goes deeper. Often, we cling to a story as if it were true, but upon closer examination, we may realize we don't have absolute certainty. This question opens the door to humility and curiosity: What if I don't know for sure? What else might be possible?

3. How do I react—what happens—when I believe that thought?

This step brings mindful awareness to your body and emotions. Notice: Does the thought cause tension in your chest, heaviness in your stomach, or a shutting down of energy? Does it isolate you from others or keep you stuck in guilt? By becoming aware of how believing the thought shapes your experience, you begin to see the cost of holding onto it.

4. Who would I be without that thought?

This is the turning point. Imagine, even for a moment, living without the burden of that belief. Who would you be—right now—without the weight of "I should have done more" or "I'll never feel joy again"? Perhaps lighter, freer, more open to love, connection, or even gratitude. This question doesn't erase grief, but it reveals the possibility of meeting grief without being trapped in the mind's harshest stories.

After moving through the four questions, Katie suggests a final step called the "turnaround"—looking at the opposite of the thought and asking if it could be as true or truer. For example, "I should have done more" might turn into "I did enough" or "They should have done more for me." This is not about blame, but about loosening the grip of one rigid perspective and seeing the wider field of truth.

Grief will still come, but when we meet our thoughts with inquiry, we find space within the storm. We discover that while pain is real, the suffering added by unquestioned thoughts is optional. In that spaciousness, compassion—for ourselves and for others—naturally grows.

You don't need to "fix" or force anything. Just sit with each question. Feel your way through it. Sometimes the mind softens just enough to make space for something truer—not a new belief, but a clearer view of reality, unfiltered by fear or habit. Letting go, in this context, doesn't mean forgetting or pretending everything's fine. It means loosening your grip on the thoughts that keep you trapped. It means returning to the real moment—the warm light on the floor, the breath rising and falling, the life that's still here, waiting for you.

Reflection

Our emotional landscape is never as simple or as predictable as we might wish. At times, we feel a consistent ache; at other times, grief rushes us and draws everything to the forefront and takes control of our focus and energy. While I ponder these themes, I have come to realize that grappling with loss—of roles, relationships, and long-held dreams—is not a sign of defeat or weakness. It is courageous and important to acknowledge what is difficult and allow ourselves to be present with the mix of emotions. Allowing space for regret or grief does not negate the joy or gratitude I feel. It adds to my sense of meaning in what matters most.

Mindfulness has helped me move closer to acceptance by making me aware of when old patterns keep me stuck. Letting go is not a one-time event but a process influenced by small moments filled with awareness, compassion, and ritual. The practices and visualizations shared offer new ways to honor change by giving permission to release things that no longer serve. I would be remiss if I did not remind you, and myself, that healing is rarely a straight line. We gradually develop a new sense of self and hold space for awareness that, with openness and a willingness to let go, we allow room for healing, connection, and fresh starts.

Chapter 5:
Relationships Reimagined

Relationships shift and morph throughout our lives. Our children move from dependence to independence, and our parents change from caregivers to those in need of care. Partners and close friends change, too. These shifts can feel odd, unsettling, or even overwhelming. We may wonder if we are still useful or needed, or what role we now play in these new relationship dynamics.

When my father moved from his retirement home to an assisted living facility, something shifted between us. He required more care, including daily nursing support and help with bathing and changing his clothes—things the retirement home could no longer provide, and I couldn't offer myself. The move was necessary and practical. But it still felt like crossing a threshold neither of us wanted to approach.

I remember sitting with him in his new room, unpacking his things while he looked around quietly. There was no crisis, just a steady, tacit acknowledgment that a new stage in his life had now begun. We had turned a corner into a different relationship. I was no longer looking after his care needs. I had to reconceptualize how to be there for him.

After a few weeks, I realized how much our relationship had been overly focused on doctors' appointments, medication schedules, and advocacy. With the loss of those opportunities, I started to lose sight of what it meant to have a simple relationship as father and son.

Mindfulness allowed me precious time to stop, to think, and to ask another question: If I was not here to fix, arrange, take care of, or protect, how could I just be? Slowly but surely, I was able to be there for him, not with answers but with presence. I learned to sit with him, to listen more intently, to watch for those small moments of connection, and to remain silent when a problem might have arisen.

Shifting Relationship Roles

Life has a way of changing the script on us, especially in our closest relationships. The roles we once knew so well—parent, partner, child, caregiver—don't stay fixed. They shift, often quietly at first, until one day we notice we've stepped into an entirely new chapter. And with each shift comes a fresh lesson in how to love.

Take grandparenting, for example. When our first grandchild arrived, we thought we knew what to do. After all, hadn't we raised children ourselves? But those early weeks of constant crying reminded us quickly that this wasn't our stage anymore. We tried offering gentle suggestions—maybe he was hungry, maybe he needed a change—but it became clear that our daughter and her partner didn't need more theories. What they needed was something much simpler: presence. A calm voice in the room. A hand on the shoulder. Someone who could sit beside them in the hard moments without trying to fix anything. I realized then that grandparenting isn't about holding the reins—it's about holding space. It's a quieter kind of love, but no less powerful.

Then came the ache of distance. Both of our children eventually moved far away, one to New Brunswick and the other to Calgary. Pride and heartache tangled together—pride in seeing them carve out their own lives, and heartache in missing the small, everyday rituals we once took for granted. No more spontaneous dinners, no quick drop-ins. We had to learn new ways to feel close: short video calls, texts, and a photo shared in the middle of the day. We learned to celebrate those little moments, realizing that presence doesn't always require being in the same room. Love can stretch across miles if you let it.

Partnerships change, too. Retirement, illness, or even just the slow passage of time can reshuffle the balance of a household. When one partner can no longer carry the groceries, the other steps in to help. When retirement brings two people together for hours they never used to share, new rhythms need to be found—sometimes in shared hobbies, sometimes in learning to give each other space. Even intimacy evolves, shifting from physical touch to words of reassurance or quieter, more subtle gestures of care. These changes aren't always easy, but they remind us that love isn't static. It adapts. It bends. It grows in new directions.

And just when you think you've settled into later life, another role reversal often arrives: caring for your own parents. Suddenly, you find yourself scheduling appointments, managing medications, or worrying about their safety. I know that when this happened, I felt like I was caught in the middle—still supporting my adult children while also caring for my aging parents.

The Power of the Pause

"Between stimulus and response, there is a space. In that space is our power to choose our response. In our response lies our growth and our freedom." These words, often attributed to Viktor Frankl, capture the heart of mindfulness. Life continually presents us with challenges—illness, loss, aging, family tensions, or the disorientation that comes with change. Often, our old conditioning rushes in first. We hear a sharp word and immediately bristle. We feel disappointment and instantly collapse into self-criticism. These automatic reactions are deeply human, but they can keep us bound to patterns of suffering.

Mindfulness helps us discover the space Frankl describes. In the very moment a trigger arises, instead of tumbling into reactivity, we learn to pause. This pause does not mean we suppress our emotions or become passive. It means we allow enough stillness to see clearly what is happening inside us. In that pause, we might notice: My chest is tightening, anger is rising, I want to shout or shut down. By naming the experience rather than being swept away by it, we begin to loosen its grip. Research shows that mindfulness practice increases emotion regulation and reduces automatic reactivity, particularly in stressful interpersonal contexts (Kemeny et al., 2012).

A Story: Pausing in Conflict

I remember a moment at the university when a conflict with a co-worker caught me off guard. In the middle of a faculty meeting, they made a comment that felt dismissive of my work. My first reaction was to hit back with an angry comment. Instead, I remembered to be mindful. I'm not sure why; it just happened. I tuned into the heat rising in my chest, a tightening in my jaw, and the urge to defend myself sharply. That space allowed something else to emerge.

I remembered the practice of the Sacred Pause. Instead of speaking, I took a breath. I noticed the flush in my body, the storyline forming in my head—they don't respect me, I need to prove myself. Just naming it in silence gave me the space I needed. In that space, I asked: What response reflects the kind of colleague I want to be? When I did speak, it was with balance and clarity. I asked if they would like to expand on their comment. The conversation shifted. Instead of spiraling into conflict, we found a way to move forward with more mutual respect.

Practice: The Sacred Pause

Here's a simple exercise to cultivate the skill of non-reactivity:

1. Notice the trigger. The next time you feel stirred by an argument, a difficult email, or an old memory—pause. Recognize: This is a moment of activation.

2. Breathe into the body. Bring attention to your breath. Inhale gently, exhale slowly. Feel your feet on the ground, the weight of your body supported by the earth.

3. Name what's happening. Silently note what you feel: "tightness in the chest," "anger," "sadness," "the urge to fix." Naming helps create space between you and the experience.

4. Ask yourself: What response here reflects who I want to be? This brings Frankl's insight alive—you are not reacting blindly, but choosing in alignment with your values.

5. Respond, or not. Sometimes the wisest choice is to wait before saying or doing anything. At other times, it may be to speak with calm clarity. Either way, you are no longer driven by habit—you are guided by awareness.

Try practicing the Sacred Pause once a day. It might be as simple as stopping before answering the phone or taking a breath before responding to your child, partner, or co-worker. Each pause strengthens the muscle of freedom and plants seeds of growth amidst life's transitions.

Mindful Communication

During life's major transitions—like negotiating caregiving duties with siblings or adjusting finances after retirement—conversations often carry extra weight. When emotions run high, communication can quickly spiral into defensiveness or misunderstanding. Mindful communication is the art of bringing awareness, presence, and compassion into dialogue, allowing us to listen and speak with greater clarity. Gregory Kramer's *Insight Dialogue* (Kramer, 2007) offers a powerful framework for doing just this, combining mindfulness with the relational field of conversation.

The practice begins with pausing. This is the simple act of stopping before speaking. This pause gives us room to notice physical signs of stress, such as a racing heart or tight shoulders, before words tumble out. Even saying aloud, "Give me just a moment to gather my thoughts," signals self-awareness and creates space for mindful choice rather than automatic reaction. This small step models that taking time before responding is not only acceptable, but wise.

Kramer's second instruction, relax, helps us soften the body and mind in the midst of dialogue. By releasing tension and breathing into the present moment, we lower defensiveness and invite openness. From this grounded state, we can then open—not only to our own experience, but to the presence of the other person. For example, when discussing shared responsibilities with siblings, we might notice our own feelings of overwhelm while also being receptive to the stress or fear they are experiencing.

Mindful communication also means expressing ourselves with honesty and care. Using "I" statements, rather than blame, invites cooperation: "I feel anxious about our finances now that I'm retired" lands very differently than "You spend too much." This gentle honesty fosters trust, even when the topic is difficult. Similarly, a parent who longs for more contact might say, "We miss hearing from you and would love to hear from you more," instead of relying on subtle digs or silence. Such clear expression prevents resentment from building up and brings people closer together.

Equally important in *Insight Dialogue* is attuning to emergence—remaining open to what unfolds rather than clinging to fixed outcomes. We don't enter the conversation with the intention of winning an argument or proving something. We're not trying to control; instead, we ask honest, open-ended questions. We bring genuine curiosity into the dialogue. This is more likely to foster mutual understanding rather than conflict.

This type of communication does not mean that conflict never happens or that agreement is automatic. It does transform the way we dialogue around difficult topics. It opens the opportunity for connection rather than division. Simply by pausing, relaxing, opening up, and listening deeply, we create space for compassion to guide our words.

Cultivating Deeper Connections

Once you have developed the foundations of mindful and compassionate communication, the next move is to rely on these skills to create even deeper emotional connections with your loved ones. When you and your partner, family member, or friend practice sincere listening and speak without judgment, you create a safe space where vulnerability, intimacy, and genuine connection can flourish (Keng et al., 2011).A practical method to foster meaningful relationships involves practicing mindfulness together. For example, preparing a meal collaboratively can serve this purpose. Before starting, both participants should agree to concentrate solely on the task at hand. Pay attention to sensory inputs such as the aroma of the ingredients and the sound of chopping. Regularly check in with one another to assess enjoyment of the activity. The goal is not to perfect the dish or complete it quickly, but to value the shared experience. If the meal burns or is undercooked, approach it with curiosity rather than blame. Accepting each other without judgment (Schuman-Olivier et al., 2020) is a significant step toward establishing a healthy and meaningful relationship.

Another way to practice mindfulness together is through nature walks. Rather than the two of you walking in silence or worrying about a distracted conversation, choose a path, and make it a "together" activity to share three things you noticed on this walk. "I noticed how the sunlight moved on that tree," or "I felt the cool air on my skin." When we share what each of us is noticing, this strengthens our capacity to notice the present moment. It also strengthens our sense of connection.

Deeper conversations are an inevitable aspect of emotional closeness. Once you have practiced open listening, you can invite your loved one to a heart-to-heart conversation. You might ask, "What made you feel most alive today?" or "What dreams have I still not heard about?" Questions like "How might I support you better right now?" also reveal your willingness to be there for them in whatever way matters. There is no need to rush into over-advising as the questions reveal themselves; the idea here is to illuminate our partner's inner world, creating a mutual feeling of being seen and understood. If someone is struggling to open up, remind them that their thoughts don't need to be overly eloquent or profound.

Like any new habit, these conversations can fade when life gets busy. Building consistency—such as reserving 15 minutes after dinner once a week—helps transform them from occasional efforts into a steady rhythm. Over time, weaving intentional practices like mindful activities, gratitude, and check-ins into everyday life allows relationships to thrive with greater understanding, resilience, and love (Schuman-Olivier et al., 2020; Keng et al., 2011).

Reflection

As I reflect on the ideas I've shared here, I'm left wondering how far transitions can alter the nature of family life in multifaceted ways. Becoming comfortable with change—whether as a parent of adult children, a partner adjusting to shifting roles, or a caregiver to aging parents—is not an easy feat. It requires adaptability and self-awareness.

In exploring compassion and staying more fluid with change, I have learned that when I pause to listen, speak honestly about my own needs (whether calm or pissed off!), and offer compassion, I can remain connected even if things are changing around me. Boundaries, I've realized, aren't about shutting people out but about creating space where everyone, including me, can grow and thrive.

What sustains us are often the small rituals: shared moments of mindfulness, tiny expressions of gratitude, or noticing one another's quiet acts of love. While seemingly minor, they keep us feeling connected to one another, and they help us soften the chaos of life together. Of course, relationships aren't always smooth—we face old issues, growing pains related to intimacy that might feel awkward, and moments of tension. Still, I believe that if we engage in honest dialogue, compassionate acceptance, and show a bit of patience with one another, we can adapt and create something new.

Looking back on these changes, I would say that all change—especially messy change—leaves a deeper connection and understanding in its wake. It's not easy to accommodate change (and it's not always pretty!), but there is always enough compassion, connection, and care to make our relationships deeper and to discover new ways of being joyful.

Chapter 6:
Renewing Identity and Purpose

Your identity is your sense of who you are, both as an individual and in relation to others and society. It includes your personal characteristics, such as your physical and mental traits, as well as the social roles you assume in family, work, and community. You might experience an identity crisis anytime you go through a life transition or find yourself in a significantly different situation or role. It can occur at any time, during adolescence, midlife, or advanced age.

My sister recently retired after 45 years working for the same organization. That's nearly half a century of waking up with intention and purpose, walking the same hallways, knowing her place, and knowing how she contributed. She invested her energy, intellect, and heart into that job. It defined her entire day, both personally and professionally.

I see her wrestling with more than just *what to do* next: She's wrestling with *who to be* next. She's not alone. So many of us conjoin our identity with what we do—especially when we've done that work for so long. Work becomes more than a job. It becomes a compass, a container, a source of meaning.

Leaving a job can bring disorientation and excitement. For some, it's so unsettling that it can be terrifying. My sister said, "I don't know who I am without it." Many of us quietly question: Who am I when titles fade, routines stop, and no one needs me the same way? This chapter takes up that question. It's about the gentle, sometimes messy, work of renewing identity and rediscovering purpose, not by clinging to the past, but by listening ahead.

Let's explore rediscovering purpose during periods of identity transition. This chapter offers practices and activities to reconnect with our passions that may have been set aside, cultivating a vision for the next stage of life. Each section provides tools for self-inquiry, including creating statements defining our values and interests, as well as identifying obstacles. We'll also explore a method to shift our perspective and guide us in showing up authentically in the next chapter of our lives.

The Identity Puzzle

For years, being a social work professor was more than a job; it was my calling and identity, like my sister's career. I was proud to be considered thoughtful, intentional, and articulate. My days included lectures, mentoring, research, and committees. Even if tiring, I was confident in this familiar role.

When I left academia, I knew it would take some time to adjust to my new life. What I didn't realize was that I would feel so empty and lost. I felt aimless, like a boat without a rudder. I remember one morning, thinking, "Now what?"

The truth is, I wasn't just missing my routines. I was missing myself, the thing I had invested everything in. For a while, I reached back out to prove I was still a person. I wrote more, I offered advice, and I pursued every opportunity to present myself as intelligent. But slowly, something else began to emerge. I recognized I could still be wise, without being a professor. I could still be of service without needing to be the expert.

Releasing that identity wasn't easy. But in that space, I began to meet a different version of myself: less confident, perhaps, but more present and aware. It was as if a new identity could be seen and heard when I let go of the thought-constructed old self and rested in present-moment awareness.

We all face ongoing life changes that challenge our self-identity. Many people identify closely with their roles as parents, professionals, or partners. According to Erik Erikson's theory of personality, adolescents face identity confusion as they form their ego identity. A parent living through an empty nest may feel lost without their children. They may question themselves, wondering what their purpose is now that they are no longer "taking care" of their children every day. On the other hand, someone who has identified their identity with their job may experience questioning, uncertainty, or anxiety about their role after transitioning to retirement or a job change. These are just a few examples of identity shifts.

Adolescence is a season of profound becoming—a time when the question "Who am I?" moves from the background to the center stage of a young person's inner life. As teens begin to step out of childhood, leaving behind family roles, early friendships, and self-definitions, they enter a phase of deep identity restructuring.

Common Signs

Here are some common signs that you might be experiencing an identity crisis:

- **Questioning who you are at your core.** You may find yourself asking: Am I really kind? Am I honest? Do I still care about the things I thought mattered most? What once felt certain about your personality, passions, or purpose suddenly feels up for debate.

- **Feeling unsettled and restless.** Identity struggles often show up as anxiety, agitation, or a vague dissatisfaction with life. The inner confusion can ripple outward, leaving you feeling uncomfortable in your own skin.

- **Shifting yourself to fit in.** You may notice yourself changing how you act depending on the situation, relationship, or environment—so much so that you're not sure what truly feels like you. While flexibility is healthy, constantly bending to please others can blur your sense of self.

- **Struggling to describe yourself.** Simple questions like "Tell me about yourself" can suddenly feel impossible to answer. What once seemed obvious now feels unclear, leaving you unsure of how to articulate your own identity.

- **Losing trust in your decisions.** When your values feel uncertain, it's easy to second-guess yourself. You may find it hard to commit to choices or regret the ones you've made, which can eat away at confidence and self-esteem.

Reframing Identity with Mindfulness

As we saw in Chapter 2, mindfulness helps us cultivate present-moment awareness—an especially valuable skill when facing identity transitions. Instead of getting stuck in self-judgment or old patterns, mindfulness provides us with the space to pause, notice, and reflect with clarity. It reminds us that our worth isn't tied to a single role or label, and that our identity is always evolving.

When significant changes evoke fear, sadness, or anxiety, mindfulness helps us respond rather than react. A few mindful breaths or a brief body scan can bring us back to the present, grounding us in our current reality. This shift enables us to view transitions not as losses, but as opportunities to evolve into new versions of ourselves.

For many, this is a chance to explore new passions or revive old ones. Some people start volunteering, learning a new skill, or returning to a forgotten hobby. For me, it was dusting off my trombone after decades of not playing. What once felt like an ending can become a blank canvas—a chance to experiment, create, and rediscover joy.

By reframing transitions in this way, we replace regret ("Why didn't I do this sooner?") with curiosity ("What can I try today?"). Mindfulness directs our attention to the possibilities right in front of us, helping us approach identity shifts with openness, resilience, and a renewed sense of self-worth.

Mindful Rediscovery of Passion

Shifting identities can lead to persistent self-questioning, leaving many feeling adrift or uncertain about what truly matters to them. Mindfulness can help by providing both the awareness and acceptance needed for authentic self-discovery. When paired with the emotional resilience skills from Chapter 8—tools that equip individuals to process disappointment and vulnerability—and adaptability strategies from Chapter 9, mindfulness cultivates a compassionate approach to exploring long-neglected interests and passions.

Interest Inventory

We begin this process by creating an interest inventory, a reflective activity that helps reestablish connections with sources of joy from previous life stages. Carve out some time to be quiet and alone and prepare as you have in other mindfulness activities.

Now, begin to gently retrieve the experiences, activities, hobbies, or subjects that, at one time, brought you joy, satisfaction, and engagement. Perhaps you enjoyed painting, playing an instrument, gardening, writing, coordinating community events, or tinkering with various things. Jot down all that comes to your mind!

Consider prompts such as:

- What did I love doing as a child before others' expectations shaped my choices?

- Which activities made me feel most like myself during early adulthood?

- When have I felt energized instead of depleted by what I was doing?

Review your list and look for patterns. Perhaps you'll discover a repeated desire for creativity, movement, social connection, or learning new skills. Noticing these themes creates a map of where passion may be waiting to be rekindled (Utley & Garza, 2011).

With greater clarity about once-loved pursuits, begin to incorporate mindful experimentation into your active daily life. Choose one activity from your list that still sparks curiosity or longing.

Approach the activity with an open mind, and permit yourself to try it without being overly focused on excelling or judging your performance. For example, if you've always loved sketching but left it behind for career obligations, gather simple supplies and devote an afternoon to drawing purely for enjoyment, not evaluation.

As you engage in the activity, note the sensory involvement: how it feels to touch the pencil on the page, the colors that appear, and the sound of a stroke pushing across the page. When finished, take a few minutes to reflect on the experience. Did you feel invigorated or frustrated? Which part felt effortless, and what parts felt difficult? Most importantly, ask yourself, "Was there a sense of freedom or playful involvement?" Writing in a journal about these questions can provide valuable insights into genuine areas of engagement (Sutton, 2022).

Natural Writing

Another method for identifying activities that you're passionate about is the natural writing method. I developed this method while writing reports for government departments. It involves posing a question and then letting whatever arises in your mind be written down. It is like brainstorming with yourself. Do not evaluate, decide, or think about any of the ideas. Simply write down whatever comes up. Before writing, focus on the physical setup of the space you are in: a comfortable spot, suitable lighting (if helpful, consider dimming the lights), and possibly music or an aromatherapy candle. Once you are settled and sitting comfortably, I encourage you to close your eyes and take three longer, deeper breaths—allowing all other thoughts of the day to drift away and enabling yourself to be fully present in the moment as best you can.

A reflective prompt that can also reveal hidden passions is to notice when you enter a state of flow—those moments when time seems to disappear. To explore this, try writing in response to the question: "When I lose track of time, I am..." Popularized by positive psychologists Mihaly Csikszentmihalyi and Jeanne Nakamura, the flow state describes a state of being fully immersed in whatever one is doing.

Next, review what you have written. Highlight recurring themes, such as being outside, collaborating with others, teaching, or crafting stories. These are clues to the states of flow where passion often resides. Try returning to this prompt weekly for a month to see how your answers evolve and to uncover less obvious sources of engagement (80 Inner Child Journal Prompts for Reparenting Yourself - Inner Child Work, 2024).

Exploring Obstacles

Alongside discovering passions, it's essential to address obstacles. Create a list of potential barriers—both external (lack of time, financial limitations, family responsibilities) and internal (self-doubt, fear of judgment, beliefs about being "too old"). Use self-reflection questions such as:

- What stories do I tell myself about why I can't pursue what I love?

- What am I most afraid might happen if I fully commit to what I love?

- Am I waiting for someone else's permission or approval to follow my passion?

- What specific resources (time, money, skills, support) do I feel I lack?

- Do I nurture myself physically and emotionally so I have the energy to pursue what I love?

- What drains my energy that I could let go of, delegate, or say "no" to?

- When was the last time I felt fully alive and engaged? What was happening?

- Have I clearly distinguished between real limitations and imagined ones?

- How might these beliefs have protected me in the past, and are they still serving me now?

Acknowledge these obstacles without self-criticism, recognizing that all barriers contain valuable information and insights. Journaling about these challenges enables increased self-understanding and the emergence of realistic next steps toward creating space for passion. Sometimes, simply naming an obstacle begins to dissolve its power, especially when addressed through a mindful lens.

Next, we will explore the obstacles. Use one page for each of these prompts, writing freely using the natural writing method for five to ten minutes on each:

- Fear: "If I pursued what I love fully, the worst thing that could happen is…"

- Doubt: "The voice inside me that tells me I can't or shouldn't says…"

- Beliefs: "Growing up, I was taught that work and passion meant…"

- Practical Barriers: "What I think I lack to move forward is…"

- Identity: "If I really changed my life to follow this love, people might see me as…"

- Energy: "What drains me and keeps me from having energy for what I love is…"

After each section, pause and circle words or phrases that stand out—the ones that feel heavy, emotional, or charged.

- Ask: "Is this an external truth, or an internal belief I've taken on?" Sometimes what looks like a wall is actually just an old story.

These practices come alive through examples drawn from real-life experiences—for instance, rediscovering the joy of pottery after children have grown up, or finding new fulfillment in hiking after years spent in a desk job. Rather than reaching for some generic vision of passion, let each mindful experiment become a gentle exploration, meeting yourself with the same curiosity and compassion you might extend to a friend. By following concrete steps—structuring your inventories, experimenting with activities, reflecting honestly, and addressing barriers mindfully—you lay the foundation for a richer understanding of your evolving self.

As you move forward, recognize that these discoveries provide the raw material for articulating your personal sense of purpose. The insights gleaned through the practices above directly inform the creation of a meaningful purpose statement, guiding your next chapter with authenticity and renewed motivation.

Developing Your Personal Purpose Statement

Many people undergo shifts in their identity, vocation, and relationships throughout their lives. In those moments, having a personal purpose statement can really help guide and ease the prior change. While you may strive for a perfect purpose statement, it's better, instead, to think about guiding phrases that connect to your current values and hopes for the future. You can refer to the values and personal commitment statement that you did in Chapter 1. This exercise will ensure that you have a compass to help you make choices confidently, even as your priorities change (How, 2024; Imbastoni, 2023).

The exercise below will guide you through creating a personal purpose statement in three stages: reflection, analysis, and creation. You can complete this process at your own pace, allowing for opportunities for self-discovery along the way.

Phase 1: Values and Strengths Inventory

In phase 1, we clarify our personal drivers. Our purpose stems from the values, strengths, and experiences that bring us to life. Set aside ten minutes to write without interruption. You might even want to start with a meditation. This phase aims to give you a better understanding of your guiding values and skills (Imbastoni, 2023).

Step-by-step instructions:

1. List your core values. Think about principles you wouldn't want to live without, such as kindness, creativity, honesty, or learning. Ask yourself: "Which values shape my decisions and relationships?"

2. Identify natural strengths. Recall activities that come easily to you or areas where others have recognized your skills. These might include listening, problem-solving, teaching, or organizing.

3. Recall sources of genuine satisfaction. Reflect on times when you felt proud or deeply content. Use prompts like: "When do I feel most alive?" and "What contributions make me proud?"

For example, your list might include curiosity, empathy, creativity, storytelling, and volunteering. You might feel most alive when mentoring young artists or helping solve community problems.

After following the three steps, reflect on: What patterns emerge among your values and strengths? Are there activities that combine several items from your lists? Where do you see an overlap between what you enjoy and what you're good at?

Phase 2: Theme Analysis

With your inventory complete, the next phase is to explore underlying themes. This step reveals connections between different parts of your life and helps clarify what matters most (How, 2024). The expected outcome is recognition of guiding threads in your experiences.

Instructions:

1. Read through your inventories and highlight words or phrases that reappear.

2. Group similar items. For example, "helping," "mentoring," and "teaching" all relate to supporting others' growth and development.

3. Notice what makes various activities meaningful: Is it the creativity involved? The sense of connection? The impact on others?

Example: Maria sees a pattern around creativity, caring, and empowering women. She links her love for art, her work at a local women's shelter, and her value of justice under a single theme of creative empowerment.

Reflection prompts:

- Which themes resonate most strongly with who you are today?

- How do these themes reflect both your history and hopes for the future?

- Which connections surprise or inspire you?

Phase 3: Statement Creation

Finally, we create a brief and motivating statement. The goal is to write an action-oriented statement, one or two sentences long, that captures your "why." It should focus on what is personally meaningful and what action follows from that (How, 2024; Imbastoni, 2023).

Guidelines:

- Keep it simple, straightforward, and short—one to two sentences.

- Use positive, action-oriented language that expresses what you stand for and how you want to act.

- Make it personally meaningful. It should spark recognition and energy within you.

- Focus on how your actions benefit yourself, others, and the world.

Examples:

- "To cultivate creativity and resilience in myself and others through mentoring."

- "To foster authentic connection and joy with family and friends."

- "To promote healing and understanding in my community through compassionate listening."

- "To use my skills to help children discover confidence and curiosity."

Read your statement and reflect on whether or not it feels energizing and true to you. Would reading it daily help anchor your decisions and actions? If not, adjust until it resonates.

Using Your Statement Effectively

It doesn't end with writing your statement. This statement is useful only if it becomes a part of your daily life. You might want to place it somewhere where you'll see it every day, such as on your bathroom mirror or in your journal. Let the statement guide your decisions. Before making any important decision, ask yourself if the decision aligns with your values (Imbastoni, 2023). Over time, you will likely refine your statement to ensure that it continues to represent what feels true and authentic to you (How, 2024).

The statement is a guide, not a set of rules. It is designed to support mindful adaptability as you enter new chapters. In the next section, you'll build on this foundation by reframing your obstacles and shifting to the possibility of sustaining your renewed sense of direction.

Shifting to Possibility

Reframe the Story

Often, the story we tell ourselves about why we can't or shouldn't do something is actually more of a hurdle than the reality of the obstacle. For example, you might tell yourself the obstacle story, "I don't have enough time." But, is this actually true? Could it be reframed as, "What if I gave ten minutes a day to this? What could that grow into?" Or perhaps you have told the obstacle story, "I might fail and embarrass myself." That's one I've told myself numerous times. What if you reframe this as, "If I fail, I'll learn something valuable. If I succeed, my life could change."

If you are journaling on this, ask, "What's another way of seeing this obstacle?"

Another thing our minds often do is imagine we have to leap across the whole canyon in one jump. Possibility opens when we take one step at a time.

- Instead of: "I have to quit my job to be a writer."

- Try: "I can write for twenty minutes three times a week and see what unfolds."

A possible journal prompt could be, "What is the smallest step I could take toward what I love this week?" Above all else, remember your purpose statement. Remember your "Why."

Obstacles shrink when the heart expands. Reconnecting with our passion and what matters most to us brings us joy, healing, creativity, or a sense of meaning. Remember that this is a process that might take time. Consider one small step you can take to move closer to what matters most to you. Ask yourself, "What habit could I let go of to create more space for my purpose and passion to manifest?"

Reflection

Looking back on what I've learned about navigating transitions, I see how much the different parts of ourselves can become attached, cut off, and then rebuilt due to changing roles and identities. Mindfulness has allowed me to meet transitions with some gentleness, as I permit myself to acknowledge my doubts and regrets without being bound by them. It feels reassuring to know that even when parts of our old identities slip away or our future looks uncertain, there is still room for exploration and growth. Taking the time to mindfully consider what energizes me, whether it's a long-lost hobby or a skill I want to cultivate, gives me a sense of direction when I feel I need it the most.

I found the process of drafting a personal purpose statement to be grounding yet hopeful. I was able to focus on my own values and my strengths, ask meaningful questions of myself, and think differently about what it means to be us moving forward. Reframing my story and shifting to the possible enabled me to move closer each day toward what matters most to me. I now consider that transitions in life aren't about endings; rather, they offer us possibilities to explore, reimagine, and reconnect with what feels real and important.

Chapter 7:
Mindfulness for Health and Aging

One thing that is certain is that, as human beings, we will face health problems in our lives, whether physical or mental. As we age, we will experience some decline in physical, cognitive, and functional abilities. Illness, pain, financial worries, and loneliness add to these challenges, and together they may increase stress.

I always thought it was comical the way older people talked about their aches and pains. I often wondered if this was what it meant to get older. Well. Here I am, at age 66. And guess what we talk about at dinner parties now?

As I continue to think through the journey through life, I've come to see my body as a kind of temperamental roommate. Some days, my body is like a personal trainer cheering me on. Other days, it's like a disgruntled companion, throwing aches and random fatigue my way. These are not simply physical shifts in my body. They begin to affect my emotional states and perspective as well.

In this chapter, I aim to explore how simple awareness and small acts of attention can help us tune in to our bodies at any age, particularly as we age. We will learn new ways to tune into our bodies and become aware of physical sensations. We will learn how to respond with compassion to our aches and pains. Overall, we will learn tools for renewal and self-care.

Mindfulness and Physical Well-Being

While Chapter 6 explored how mindful rediscovery of passions supports identity renewal, we now examine how mindful attention to the body strengthens this transformation through improved physical well-being. The journey toward self-discovery flourishes when it is grounded in a keen awareness of one's physical state, as the mind and body are interconnected partners in shaping our sense of possibility, energy, and self-worth.

During life transitions, stress can subtly rob vitality, especially as the demands seem excessive. Chronic stress can negatively affect all our body systems. For example, it can increase blood pressure, disrupt hormonal balance, and impair immune function. This manifests as increased risk for not just heart disease and diabetes but also a host of other conditions (Jamil et al., 2023).

Mindfulness disrupts this destructive cycle by training attention to focus on the present moment. It can gently help the body break free from the automatic activation of the sympathetic nervous system—the stressful "fight-or-flight" response—by engaging the parasympathetic nervous system, often referred to as the body's relaxing "rest-and-digest" response. With regular mindfulness practice, the breathing slows, muscle tension is released, and heart rate steadies. This change leads to measurable health benefits, including reduced hypertension and lower cholesterol levels, among others.

In my experience, restorative sleep is another outcome of mindfulness. For many, sleep is difficult because racing thoughts from the day or unresolved stress keep them awake. Mindfulness promotes a gentle unwinding before bedtime. Mindfulness practices, such as slow, deep breaths or a simple body scan, can help increase awareness of where tension is stored in each muscle, triggering the nervous system to recognize that it is safe to relax. With the mind spinning less and the body relaxing, sleep becomes easier and deeper.

Physiological Benefits of Mindfulness

Mindfulness also offers physiological benefits. The practice helps us become more alert and relaxed. People who incorporate mindfulness into their nightly routines often find that they fall asleep more quickly, wake up less frequently during the night, and rise in the morning feeling more refreshed. Over time, you'll more clearly notice that the fog of fatigue lifts, irritability lessens, and your focus improves throughout the day. Consistent good sleep can ease problems like insomnia and support your body's healing processes, especially as you age (Jamil et al., 2023).

The cardiovascular and immune systems directly benefit from the steady application of mindfulness. For the heart, mindfulness techniques help maintain healthy blood pressure by calming the body's stress response and reducing inflammatory signals that damage blood vessels. Studies show that people who practice mindfulness also typically have a better cholesterol profile, with a higher percentage of HDL, which is associated with a reduced risk of heart disease (Jamil et al., 2023).

Mindfulness can have a profoundly deeper impact on inflammation in the body, extending beyond the heart. By lowering levels of stress hormones, such as cortisol, and reducing the production of pro-inflammatory cytokines, these practices help guard against illnesses ranging from diabetes to arthritis.

The immune system also grows more robust. Regular meditation has been linked to better regulation of immune responses, making the body less vulnerable to infections and slowing the progression of chronic diseases. There is even emerging evidence that mindfulness may affect aging on a genetic level, supporting the maintenance of telomere length, which is crucial for healthy cell division and longevity (Jamil et al., 2023; Berk et al., 2017). Integrating mindful movement, such as yoga or walking meditations, further complements these effects by marrying physical activity with conscious presence, strengthening the heart, lungs, and overall stamina.

Body awareness, mindfulness in its most elemental form, brings new insight into the subtle language of the body. By turning inward and observing sensations without judgment, people learn to distinguish between actual physical needs and passing urges. This skill helps identify signs of hunger, thirst, fatigue, or even early symptoms of illness far earlier than before. Prompt responses allow people to adjust their behavior as needed: drink if your mouth is dry, stretch if your muscles are tense, or consult a physician if necessary.

As we grow older, this heightened awareness encourages us to adopt preventative self-care. For example, rather than resisting or numbing ourselves when we experience pain or discomfort, we tune into what the body is asking for and respond. That might mean standing up every 30 minutes after sitting at a desk or recognizing when we've overexerted ourselves. As a writer, I would sit for hours at the computer, not noticing that my back was seizing up. Now, I am more likely to notice. I even bought a standing desk and a small walking treadmill to practice self-care.

Through these moments of attunement, self-compassion grows in tandem with resilience, reinforcing the journey of personal transformation begun in Chapter 6. When physical health is tended through mindful care, the pursuit of passion and identity becomes all the more vibrant, grounded in a body that feels seen, respected, and alive (Jamil et al., 2023; Berk et al., 2017).

A Deeper Body Scan Meditation

After exploring how mindfulness increases emotional resilience in the previous chapter, the benefits of this practice should be clear. Integrating body scan meditation into your daily routine can help you reconnect with your body, fostering both acceptance and curiosity about your feelings from moment to moment (O'Bryan, 2021; Young, 2023). We touched on this in an earlier chapter. Let's go deeper with this core practice.

You can perform a body scan meditation by listening to a recorded guided meditation or by guiding yourself using the provided instructions. For guided meditations, I recommend exploring Insight Timer. For my recorded body scan, search for "A Guided Body Scan for Healing and Presence" or browse for my name to access over 40 tracks available for free. This meditation is suitable for someone trying a body scan for the first time. It contains many instructions that an experienced meditator might not find useful. For those who are more familiar with the body scan, I recommend the "Guided Body Awareness Meditation: Three Centers" on Insight Timer.

Here are the instructions in case you want to self-guide. Choose your space and decide whether you're more comfortable lying down on a mat, couch, or bed, or sitting upright with both feet on the floor. The key is for your body to be supported yet alert. If you're sitting, keep your back straight but not stiff, allowing your shoulders to relax naturally. Lying down, uncross your arms and legs, letting them rest comfortably at your sides. Place a pillow under your knees or neck if needed for support. Set a timer for ten to thirty minutes.

Begin by closing your eyes or lowering your gaze. Take several slow, deep breaths, feeling your chest and belly expand and soften as you inhale and exhale. Let each exhale soothe your muscles and allow your attention to settle in the present moment. Bring your focus gently to your feet and toes. Notice sensations such as temperature—are they cool or warm? Feel the texture of socks, the weight of blankets, tingling, numbness, or even nothing at all. Spend about twenty to thirty seconds here, simply noticing without trying to change anything. Imagine scanning these areas with a gentle light, illuminating whatever is present. Remember that a blank is okay, too.

Shift attention up to your ankles, then to your calves and shins. Notice the pressure against the surface beneath you, whether it feels tight, pulsing, or relaxed. Continue guiding your awareness upward: knees, thighs, pelvis, abdomen, lower back. In each region, pause to notice and explore what sensations are present. You might feel clothing brushing against your skin, subtle aches, warmth, or perhaps emotional echoes that surface as tension or release (Kabat-Zinn, 2009, as cited in O'Bryan, 2021). Allow your breath to anchor you whenever your mind wanders.

Move next to your chest and upper back. Notice the rhythm of your breathing, your heartbeat, or the pressure where your body meets the floor. Let awareness flow into your shoulders, arms, and hands. Sense any tightness or ease, aches or tingles—each sensation is welcome, and none is better than another. You may identify with a river flowing steadily downstream, touching every rock, plant, or pebble. Your attention similarly flows through each body part.

Bring attention to your neck, throat, jaw, face, and finally, the top of your head. Explore sensations like warmth, itching, numbness, and the touch of hair or air. Hold your awareness here for a short time, noticing any sensations that arise. Whenever you drift into thought or judgment, whether wishing for different sensations or becoming impatient, gently return your focus to the present area without judgment. It's normal for your mind to wander; each return is integral to the training.

After scanning each part individually, expand your attention to include your whole body. Notice any sensations in the body. Imagine your breath flowing at the top of your head and flowing down through your body. On the exhale, imagine the air flowing back up from the feet to the top of the head.

Bring curiosity to how you feel in the present moment. Perhaps calmer, lighter, or more attuned to comfort and discomfort. There is no right or wrong outcome. The body scan isn't meant to "fix" you but to help you become friends with your body's ever-changing landscape. Over time, regular practice not only supports emotional steadiness but also enriches your understanding of movement and stillness in everyday life, laying the groundwork for mindful movement practices.

If you notice difficulty staying focused, remember this is entirely natural. Some days your mind will race, or your legs or back may ache. Try shorter scans or focus on just one or two areas. Use props or cushions to support injuries or stiffness, adjusting your position as needed. The value lies in showing up and paying attention, not in doing things perfectly. With time, each practice weaves together greater body awareness and resilience, thereby enhancing well-being as one ages (Young, 2023; O'Bryan, 2021).

Exercise as Mindful Movement

When I feel anxious or overwhelmed by change, I turn to movement. Not to escape, but to come back into my body. Yoga has been beneficial over the years, and there's one practice I return to again and again: Sun Salutations. This simple sequence of twelve poses moves the spine in almost every direction. It stretches the body, steadies the breath, and settles the mind. It's not about performance. It's about rhythm, flow, and getting unstuck, physically and mentally.

As we age, this type of full-body, breath-connected movement becomes even more crucial. It supports circulation, digestion, and energy levels. More than that, it reminds me I have a body. A place to land when life feels ungrounded. If you're new to Sun Salutations, there's no need to overthink it. Search "Healthline sun salutation" and you'll find a guide that walks you through it. Try one round. Then another. See what shifts for yourself.

Mindful movement offers something other than typical exercise. Rather than just counting steps or repetitions, mindful movement is movement with non-judgmental, present-moment awareness. This means moving with intention, paying attention to each sensation, and tuning into the body's needs in that moment. Exercise can sometimes become rote or habitual, but mindful movement means being actively engaged in each stretch and breath (Hoshaw, 2022; Jones, 2024). It includes the elements of noticing where your body is on a "feeling" spectrum, the quality of your breath, and your emotions during the activity. This is a shift in viewing exercise as an experience to cultivate both your body and your mind, rather than an item on a to-do list.

Depending on your age, not all movement practices are suitable for everyone. Walking meditation or Tai Chi are good alternatives. The advantage of walking is that it is accessible to more people, doesn't require equipment, and can be done either outside or inside. You can feel the ground beneath your feet with each step. You can notice the motion of your arms swinging, the movement around you, and maybe feel the breeze on your face.

If you would like to explore yoga as a mindful movement practice, I have recorded two guided yoga sessions: "MBSR Yoga Series 1 Laying Down" and "MBSR Yoga Series 2 Standing". Both are available on Insight Timer. Simply search for the title with my name, Steven Hick.

Tai Chi also offers a gentle approach to movement. Tai Chi employs slow, flowing movements that emphasize safe and balanced mobility. Each motion is connected to an inhale or exhale, which increases stability and flexibility. Swimming provides buoyancy that reduces stress on joints and is particularly beneficial for individuals with arthritis, limited range of motion, or mobility challenges. In the water, you are weightless and can move freely, using the water to support you as you move.

Choosing an exercise level can depend on your level of fitness, any existing medical conditions, and your personal interests. If a type of movement creates pain or discomfort, listen to your body. You can adjust the movement to suit your needs or opt to practice an alternative exercise. Finding a match between the practice and your own capacities helps keep mindful movement safe, fun, and rewarding (Hoshaw, 2022).

Observing bodily sensations brings the benefits of body scan meditation into action. As you move, check in with your feet, legs, arms, back, and neck. Feel the muscles contract and relax, the joints flex and extend, and notice any warmth or tightness that develops. Acknowledge areas of ease and note any areas of discomfort. Bringing attention to these details helps prevent mindless pushing through pain and allows you to care for your body with respect. When thoughts drift toward goals or self-criticism, gently refocus on the current moment, your body's sensations, your movements, and the space around you, even if only for a few seconds at a time (Jones, 2024).

By incorporating mindful pauses, you are adding another layer of protection for your well-being. Before starting your exercise, take a few quiet breaths and conduct a self-check on your feelings and readiness. While you're moving, take the opportunity to pause at natural stopping points, such as after a lap, a set, or every five minutes of movement. In those moments, take some time to reflect on what your body is telling you. Are you breathing comfortably? Did you feel strain or fatigue? Is your heart rate manageable? These and other physical and mental indicators tell you when to adjust your approach.

If you notice your knees are beginning to ache while walking, which may be due to increased intensity, try walking slowly, decreasing the length of your stride, or walking on a softer surface. If you notice fatigue setting in during a Tai Chi session, you can rest for a moment or two, or repeat a simple movement until you feel ready to continue. The changes are responding to what your body is telling you, which is a better means of minimizing the chances of injury and helping you stay consistent over time (Hoshaw, 2022).

Cultivating an appreciation for your body becomes easier with mindful movement. When negative self-talk arises—such as discouragement over stiffness or frustration with slower progress—shift your focus to gratitude. Celebrate small milestones, such as being able to walk a little farther, complete a new swim stroke, or master one more Tai Chi movement. Shift the focus from criticism to acknowledgment of resilience, adaptability, and endurance. After finishing the movement, linger in moments of satisfaction. Thank your body for its efforts and recognize that every movement supports your overall health.

The heightened body awareness developed through the body scan provides a good transition into mindful movement. Because you're already practiced in tuning into subtle physical signals, like tension, comfort, and breath, you can notice them more easily while moving. (Hoshaw, 2022; Jones, 2024).

The Science Behind Body Awareness in Aging and Health

As people age, changes in physical ability, chronic health issues, and increased sensitivity to pain can affect daily life and emotional well-being. Research indicates that mindfulness practices, including body scans and mindful movement, can influence how older adults respond to these changes. These practices provide measurable benefits for both the body and mind.

Neuroscientific studies suggest that body scan practices can enhance interoceptive awareness, the ability to recognize internal bodily sensations. Regular focus on bodily sensations has been linked to reduced activity in brain areas associated with overthinking and self-criticism, while increasing activity in regions responsible for sensory awareness and attention to the present moment (Farb et al., 2013). These findings imply that body-focused mindfulness lessens the "secondary suffering" caused by negative thoughts about aging or illness. This allows individuals to face discomfort with greater acceptance.

Mindful movement practices, such as yoga and Tai Chi, have been extensively studied in older populations. Meta-analyses have shown that yoga significantly improves the quality of life, balance, flexibility, and mental health in older adults, while also reducing anxiety and depressive symptoms (Cramer et al., 2019). Similarly, Tai Chi has been shown to reduce the risk of falls, improve mobility, and enhance cardiovascular and cognitive function in older adults (Wayne et al., 2014). These practices not only strengthen the body but also enhance self-efficacy and perceived control, which are crucial psychological resources for navigating the challenges of aging (Li et al., 2014).

Physiological research has highlighted lower stress markers, such as cortisol, and improved immune function among older adults who engage in body-based mindfulness practices (Black & Slavich, 2016).

These changes not only mitigate the physical effects of aging but also help manage chronic illnesses. Overall, the evidence suggests that body-focused mindfulness transforms how older adults experience pain, loss of function, and vulnerability. It shifts their experience from one of decline to one of adaptability and growth.

Reflection

Reflecting on the practices in this chapter, I realize that mindfulness is more than just "being present." Mindfulness is also a way to listen to my body and act in ways that align with those messages. For example, practicing body scan meditation revealed to me the discoveries beneath the habitual actions of everyday activities—sensations of slight pains, small pleasures, and quiet messages that are often overlooked. It feels reassuring to know that my moment-by-moment awareness helps protect my heart, promotes better sleep, and ultimately enhances my overall well-being.

Bringing mindfulness into movement has been a life-changing learning experience for me. Activities such as walking, cycling, or yoga became richer when I focused on the sensations in my body, instead of worrying about whether I was doing the movement correctly. Instead of treating exercise like a chore, I've learned to see it as an invitation to be kind to my body, especially on days when energy is low or stiffness appears. Adjusting pace or pausing out of respect for what I'm feeling makes long-term well-being more possible. Little by little, I began to notice an increasing appreciation for all that my body endures and achieves day after day. As I cultivate mindful acceptance and self-compassion, I feel like I am building a healthy foundation that supports both physical strength and a renewed sense of who I am becoming.

Chapter 8:
Emotionally Resilient Living

One of my meditation retreats was a seven-day silent loving-kindness retreat with Michelle McDonald at the Insight Meditation Society. I entered the retreat anticipating some degree of peace, and maybe some clarity. I did not expect to feel a surge of anger hit me on the fifth day. It was raw, hot, and very disorienting. During my meeting with Michelle, I communicated to her, "I was never an angry person until I started meditating."

She didn't flinch or seem surprised. Instead, she asked gently, "What happens next when anger arises?" I didn't know. Nobody had thought to ask me that. I'd always avoided anger my entire life. I numbed and avoided the feeling through distraction, drugs, or alcohol. But now, Michelle was presenting the idea that I could be with the anger and observe it. And once I did, something shifted. I realized I was not just angry; I was angry about my anger. I was judging the emotion and feeding it more anger.

That retreat taught me an important lesson: resilience does not come from pushing something away. Resilience comes from moving toward it and eventually through it with curiosity. Years later, I began to see the same idea in smaller, tangible moments in everyday experiences. I started to notice, for example, the quiet sense of anxiety that arose for me every time I received a phone call after 8:00 p.m. It took me a while to realize, but most of those calls contained family information, which caused a wave of anxiety. Once I tuned into the anxiety I felt—the tightness in my stomach, the rush of adrenaline, and the increase in my heartbeat—it helped me understand the story behind my reactions. With that understanding, I found a little more space and a little more freedom.

This chapter is about that space. It is about being able to meet our emotions, especially the big, messy, or difficult feelings, with openness rather than fear. Resilience is not about *not* feeling; it is about feeling wisely.

Emotional Intelligence

For most of my life, I struggled to recognize my emotional ups and downs. I would feel calm, and then suddenly overwhelmed. I was often taking action before I was fully conscious of what triggered the charged emotions. I would say things that caused more hurt and stress.

At first, I didn't understand why this was happening. I would blame myself for being oversensitive, not good at relationships, and sometimes even antisocial. Social situations drained me, despite my longing for friendships and social connections. Things began to make sense later in life, when I realized I was on the autism spectrum. That discovery provided me with much-needed context, but it didn't give me the tools I needed to navigate my emotions or relationships with greater ease.

What has always helped is mindfulness—specifically, emotional intelligence practices. These practices let me slow down and observe what was happening inside without judgment. Eventually, I could identify my feelings in the moment and recognize how often my reactions were rooted in old, unconscious patterns. I began to see that emotional intelligence could provide a method for accepting and being with whatever thoughts and emotions arose. I realized that I could bring curiosity, clarity, and care to my social interactions. And perhaps most importantly, I learned to stop trying to "fix" my feelings and began to listen to them.

Emotional intelligence is our ability to recognize, manage, and express our emotions in a thoughtful and responsible manner. It is a skill that can be developed with deliberate effort, especially at times during our lives when relationship dynamics are changing, roles are shifting, and internal transitions feel heightened. Another practice to develop our emotional intelligence is to focus on noticing our feelings, identifying their causes, and practicing empathy throughout the week. Here are a few easy, practical tools.

- Emotional Check-In: Pause during your day and ask yourself, "What am I feeling right now?" Naming your emotions builds awareness and gives you a chance to respond instead of react.

- Pause and Breathe: When strong feelings arise, take three slow breaths before speaking or acting. This space helps break automatic habits and invites more skillful choices. This trains non-reactivity, the capacity to notice without immediately acting.

- Practice Empathy: Listen with presence. Instead of jumping in with advice, try acknowledging what someone else feels. A phrase like, "That sounds really tough," can be deeply healing.

- Journal Reflection: Each evening, write a few sentences about an emotional moment from your day. What were you feeling? How did you respond? What might you do differently next time?

- Self-Compassion: When difficult feelings arise, remind yourself that this is a natural part of being human. You're not failing by feeling—you're living. Speak to yourself with the same kindness you'd offer a friend.

With time, these small daily practices build a larger capacity for emotional steadiness. You may find that your emotions begin to feel less overwhelming and more like signals or essential information to help guide you forward. Whether or not you identify as neurodivergent, cultivating emotional intelligence is one of the most empowering steps you can take to enhance your well-being. It brings more honesty to your relationships, insight into your choices, and a sense of grace to your everyday life. Emotional resilience isn't about being unaffected. It's about being deeply connected and still steady.

Understanding Emotional Triggers

We have already explored how mindfulness can enhance your physical health by regulating the stress response in Chapter 7, and we will build on that foundation here as we examine how mindfulness fosters emotional resilience and helps manage emotional triggers.

Emotional triggers are the small sparks that ignite a significant emotional response. They are quick and often sudden. They're different for everyone, but here are some common ones I've seen (and lived myself):

- Criticism. Even small comments can sting and leave you defensive or ashamed.

- Being ignored. Feeling unseen or unheard can evoke feelings of anger or sadness.

- Unmet expectations. When plans fall through or someone lets you down, frustration can rise quickly.

- Loss of control. Situations where you can't steer the outcome often trigger anxiety.

- Old wounds. Past hurts, like rejection or failure, can resurface in present moments.

- Conflict. Arguments, even about small things, can seem more significant if they touch on deeper fears.

- Change. New routines, moves, or even joyful transitions can stir up insecurity.

The key with triggers isn't to try to avoid them. We usually can't, anyway. It's about noticing them early, before the resulting emotion carries you away. Once you know your patterns, you can pause, breathe, and respond with more clarity.

Life's transitions, such as the "empty nest" when children leave home, caring for aging parents, changes at work, health scares, or shifts in relationships, can all trigger emotions like feeling left behind, fear, loneliness, or questioning one's role and worth.

When we experience an emotional trigger, our brain engages the stress-response cycle. Our body reacts with increased heart rate, muscles become tight, and breathing becomes shallow. These physical sensations are the body's way of preparing itself to deal with what it interprets to be a threat. If we aren't aware or do not intervene, we may automatically behave in ways that isolate ourselves from others, react angrily to a perceived threat, or avoid engaging in important discussions. As time passes, these reactions become habitual.

Mindfulness helps interrupt the stress-response cycle. It directs us to bodily sensations and thoughts, and teaches us to notice the creeping sensations of a trigger before it results in a full-blown emotional storm. For example, suppose we feel slighted when a young colleague is praised for their work. In that case, we can employ mindfulness, notice the trigger, and intentionally respond to the experience rather than react reflexively and defensively. In this short-lived moment of awareness, we have a deliberate choice, consistent with our values, to elicit feedback, celebrate the other's accomplishment, or ignore the trigger.

When we can step back and see our triggers, they lose their power over us. I like to say that they lose their juice. Then, they can be viewed as opportunities for growth. For example, a co-worker criticizing my work with personal attacks can trigger defensiveness and anger. When the trigger is named and seen, it allows me to pause and respond with clarity and wisdom instead of thrashing out and getting even. I can pause and reflect to consider, "What is the co-worker trying to say?" or "What are reasonable next steps for my growth?" By facing each trigger mindfully, what could have been stressful encounters are transformed into opportunities for personal growth and development.

STOP Method for Managing Strong Emotions

Being able to tune into our minds and bodies strengthens our ability to notice, process, and recover from intense emotions, grounding us in the present rather than leaving us swept up in automatic reactions. This foundation becomes particularly important during transitions—times when children leave home or work roles shift, often stirring up feelings of loss, anxiety, or excitement. Recognizing these natural responses with acceptance helps create emotional steadiness (Mayo Clinic, 2022; Lindsay et al., 2018).

One practice that supports this shift is the STOP technique. Its purpose is to interrupt automatic emotional cycles, creating a moment of awareness between a triggering event and your response. For example, if you receive unexpected news about your job, your heart might race, and frustration may flare.

Here's a breakdown of the STOP method:

- S - Stop: When emotions take over, the first step is simple: pause, even for a few seconds. Interrupt the automatic flow of thoughts and actions. If you feel anger, fear, or frustration rising, stop and take a moment to calm yourself. Don't react. Don't say the first thing that comes to mind. Don't move a muscle. Just hold still.

- T - Take a Breath: Notice your breath. Feel the air moving in and out. Let this simple noticing steady you. When big emotions arise, clear thinking often doesn't come immediately. Give yourself time. Step back from the situation. Stay with your breath until the intensity softens. Most of life does not require instant answers. Rarely do we need split-second decisions. Let your breath buy you space. From that calmer place, choose how to respond.

- O - Observe: Notice what's happening inside you—your thoughts, feelings, and body. Let them be there without judgment. Now widen your attention. Look around. Who's here? What are people saying or doing? Pay attention without rushing to label it good or bad. Negative thoughts may pop up fast. Remember, they're old patterns, not facts. Before you decide, pause. Gather what's real. See your options clearly. Then choose your next step with care.

- P - Proceed: Based on your observations, make a conscious choice about how to proceed. This might involve continuing with what you were doing, adjusting your approach, or taking a completely different action.

The STOP method provides a pause that interrupts old patterns and reduces the rush to react impulsively. Many people initially struggle to remember to practice STOP, especially during heated moments. I found that the more I practiced, the more likely I was to do it in those stressful or heated moments. As you practice, you may notice a growing ability to reflect before responding, fewer regrets after stressful conversations, and a sense of inner control even during upheaval (Mayo Clinic, 2022; Lindsay et al., 2018).

Breathing Techniques

Building on the pause, a breathing method can help calm the nervous system and move you out of fight-or-flight mode. When emotions spike, a breathing exercise can help ease tension. Two techniques that I have found helpful are Belly Breathing and Box Breathing.

How to Practice Belly Breathing (Diaphragmatic Breathing):

- Place hands: Place one hand on your abdomen.

- Inhale deeply: Breathe in slowly through your nose, allowing your abdomen to rise as you fill your lungs with air.

- Exhale slowly: Breathe out gently through your nose, feeling your abdomen fall as you release the air.

- Focus: Pay attention to the sensations in your abdomen with each breath, allowing the rest of the body to relax.

How to Practice Box Breathing:

1. Inhale: Breathe in slowly and deeply through your nose for a count of four, feeling your lungs fill with air.

2. Hold: Hold your breath for a count of four.

3. Exhale: Breathe out slowly and thoroughly through your mouth for a count of four, releasing all the air from your lungs.

4. Hold: Hold your breath for a count of four.

5. Repeat: Continue this cycle, imagining you are tracing a box.

As you repeat these breathing exercises, you may notice a gentle slowing of your heartbeat, relaxed shoulders, and clearer thinking.

Early on, some people feel restless or like they can't "breathe right." It's helpful to start with just two or three rounds and gradually increase the number of rounds over time. If sitting still feels agitating, try this while walking or swaying lightly. Over time, you may notice progress in the form of a quicker return to calm after stress, fewer headaches, and an increased ability to ride out tough feelings without becoming overwhelmed. These changes come from activating the body's parasympathetic response—the calming system, as described in Chapter 7 (Mayo Clinic, 2022).

Self-Compassion

Self-compassion is key here. Notice how you speak to yourself when life feels rough. Life's significant transitions often stir up a harsh inner voice. You might hear things like, "I should be handling this better," or "What's wrong with me?"

The practice here is simple, but not always easy. Notice when that voice shows up. Pause. Then try offering yourself a kinder response. It can be a simple statement, such as, "This is hard, and that's okay," or "It's normal to feel lost right now. I'm doing my best." At first, these words may feel stiff or unnatural. That's normal, too. With practice, they start to land more deeply.

If compassion feels out of reach, imagine what you'd say to a close friend in the same spot. You'd likely offer patience, encouragement, or just presence. Try turning that same warmth toward yourself. Over time, this slight shift can help ease rumination, soften shame, and provide you with more space to learn from setbacks instead of being overwhelmed by them.

Mindful Movement and Processing Emotions

As we explored in Chapter 7 on aging and health, bringing mindfulness into physical movement benefits us in countless ways. One of the most profound is its ability to help us process emotions that often become stored in the body. Many of us carry stress, sadness, fear, or anger even without realizing it, and these emotions can show up as physical tension—tight shoulders, a clenched jaw, a heavy chest, or a knot in the stomach. Over time, these patterns of holding can become so familiar that we stop noticing them, even as they subtly shape our feelings on a day-to-day basis.

Mindful movement enables us to sense where emotions are "trapped" and gently bring them into awareness. When we notice these signals with curiosity instead of judgment, something begins to shift. For example, you might realize that your shoulders are constantly lifted toward your ears, a subtle sign that you're bracing against stress. By slowly and intentionally lowering and relaxing them during movement, you are not only releasing muscular tension but also signaling to your nervous system that it is safe to let go. In this way, the physical act of relaxing the body also becomes an emotional release.

The science supports this connection. Research on mindfulness and movement has shown that practices such as yoga, Tai Chi, and even mindful walking reduce physiological markers of stress, including cortisol, while increasing activity in brain regions that regulate emotion (Cramer et al., 2019; Wayne et al., 2014).

This suggests that what we experience as "relaxing the shoulders" or "softening the jaw" is more than just a muscular adjustment—it is part of a larger process of resetting the body's stress response and improving emotional balance.

With practice, mindfulness in movement helps us tune into the body's messages more quickly and respond with kindness. Each time we notice tension in our body and consciously soften and release it, we are training ourselves to let go not only of physical tension but also of the emotional burdens that accompany it. Over time, this builds resilience, allowing us to carry the inevitable stresses of life with greater ease and less accumulation of hidden weight. Choose a movement that feels accessible and enjoyable, such as yoga, Tai Chi, mindful walking, or gentle stretching. Individuals with mobility challenges can adapt movements to suit their specific needs. You may want to consider revisiting the guided yoga practices that I recorded on Insight Timer, "MBSR Yoga Series 1 Laying Down" and "MBSR Yoga Series 2 Standing" if yoga resonates with you.

If emotions become overwhelming during mindful movement, pause and take a moment to regroup. Remember that your breath is always there as a mindfulness anchor. Use it to ground yourself and come back to the present moment. Focus on self-compassion rather than on achieving any end result.

RAIN Meditation

The RAIN practice is another effective way to manage overwhelming emotions. In that case, I invite you to practice a meditation available on Insight Timer called "Let It RAIN: A Mindful Path Through Difficult Emotions." Michelle McDonald, an early meditation teacher of mine, developed a process called RAIN for dealing with emotions. RAIN stands for:

- *Recognizing* the emotion

- *Allowing* the emotion to be present

- *Investigating* the thoughts and sensations associated with the emotion

- *Not* identifying with the emotion

Some mindfulness teachers have added an S at the end to emphasize self-compassion. In the guided meditation I recorded, the "N" stands for "Nurture." You are invited to nurture the part of you that feels tender or vulnerable with kindness and compassion.

Each of these practices helps navigate emotional turmoil.

Self-Forgiveness and Forgiveness of Others

Self-forgiveness practice begins with self-acceptance. Self-acceptance is a common theme in mindfulness-based interventions such as Mindfulness-Based Stress Reduction (MBSR).

Begin your self-forgiveness by settling into your usual meditation posture. Start by recalling a situation where you were really hard on yourself—one of those moments where self-criticism and self-judgment were rampant. From there, repeat to yourself a simple phrase such as "I forgive myself for the mistakes I have made. May I be at peace." If obstacles arise, such as resistance or guilt (and they will sometimes), that is okay. Just recognize the obstacle and return to the phrase.

Research suggests that self-acceptance and self-forgiveness practices can interrupt rumination and regret habits, freeing up energy for moving forward (Keng et al., 2011; Oh et al., 2022).

To cultivate forgiveness of others, you can try loving-kindness meditations. In this meditation, we direct loving kindness specifically toward the person we feel has wronged us. You can think of someone with whom you are angry, or someone from whom you harbor significant resentment. Then, from there, either in writing or out loud, practice loving-kindness by saying, "May you be free from suffering. May you find peace." Eventually, even if we feel discomfort or anger at first, the hurt we feel dissipates, and kindness emerges.

With continued practice, mindfulness-based forgiveness can help reduce emotional distress. It enhances psychological well-being because it enables us to acknowledge and experience difficult feelings, identify old wounds, and eventually and intentionally release them (Oh et al., 2022). In other words, once we make space for a forgiving activity, we free ourselves for emotional freedom and enhance our positive connection with ourselves as well as with others.

Shifting From "Why Me?" to "What Can I Learn?"

Let's face it, life's big transitions almost always bring some discomfort. Too often, we see that discomfort as a sign of failure, or we stress about the fact that it's even there. But mindfulness gives us a way to change our relationship to that discomfort.

Take job loss as an example. It's normal to feel shame, fear, or self-doubt. These emotions can be overwhelming. Mindfulness doesn't make them disappear, but it does give us tools to face them. One simple step is to pause and name what has happened, and then name the emotions you're feeling—without blame, without harsh judgment.

From there, you can begin to ask a different question: "What can I learn from this? What new path or strength might this open up for me?" Shifting the inner dialogue from "Why me?" to "What can I learn?" opens space for curiosity instead of self-criticism. Writing down your reflections or simply holding them in mind can help you approach even painful transitions with openness.

Here's a simple example:

"I lost my job. I feel scared, uncertain, and discouraged. But I can update my résumé. I can reach out to people I trust. I can apply for new roles."

This small act of reframing starts to rebuild confidence. It's not pretending everything is fine—it's recognizing that, alongside the fear, you still have choices and strengths you can lean on. Research shows that people who practice this kind of mindful reframing often report higher optimism and adaptability (Moss et al., 2017; Xi et al., 2015; Oh et al., 2022).

Another powerful tool is intentionally noticing joy, even in hard times. These don't have to be big or dramatic moments—sometimes it's the first sip of coffee in the morning, sunlight through a window, or laughter with someone you love. Try pausing twice a day to notice something that brings you ease or comfort. If you like, write down three of these small joys in a gratitude journal at night. Over time, this practice rewires your brain to see more of the good, even when life feels heavy (Epel et al., 2019; Jiga et al., 2018).

Gratitude won't erase pain, but it can soften its grip. It balances out the stress and brings more steadiness to the heart. And when gratitude is shared—with a kind word, a thank-you, or a small gesture—it deepens your connection with others.

Mindfulness, reframing, and joy-seeking work together to create an emotional anchor. They don't stop the waves of life's challenges, but they help you ride them with more balance, resilience, and hope.

Reflection

Mindfulness is not about pretending that aches and pains don't exist. It's about not resisting them and paying attention. I've noticed that my body is constantly changing and can't do the things that it once did. What's crucial for me is to listen to the signals that my body continuously sends. I really bring curiosity to my physical body sensations. By listening in this way, I'm not fighting against aging; I'm learning to befriend it.

What comforts me most is that these small, mindful acts have a ripple effect. Each pause, each scan, each mindful movement not only eases stress but also strengthens resilience, deepens gratitude, and helps me live with more steadiness. Aging does bring aches and groans, but if we don't make the body a source of struggle, and instead listen, it can become a teacher and a bridge to presence and joy.

Chapter 9:
The Art of Letting Go and Beginning Again

When our daughter left home, I was shocked by how much it impacted me. I had already experienced this once when our son, Justin, left for college, so I thought I was prepared. But Kristina was our youngest and the last to leave home, and this time it was different. Little things upset me, such as the empty chair at the dinner table, the mostly empty laundry basket, and the quietness of the car that once was filled with music or endless conversation. I felt unanchored and unsettled.

Being empty nesters wasn't the transition I expected. It was emotional and unsettling. I found that many of my daily routines had disappeared, leaving me feeling empty. I felt like I lost my sense of purpose. Many of the things I used to do were gone, leaving me unsure of what to do throughout the day. I discovered that mindfulness could play a key role in navigating this significant transition. Once I began to notice my sorrow and accept it, I was no longer overwhelmed by it. I became curious, asked new questions, loosened my grip on what had been, and considered new possibilities.

Have you noticed yourself wishing you could handle unexpected life changes more gracefully? Many of us feel uneasy when a major transition happens. Life's big changes can be extremely unsettling, especially when they bring uncertainty and anxiety. Many questions arise: How do I reconnect when my life feels out of control? How can I respond instead of react? Some researchers have suggested that these major transitions are among the most stressful events in a person's life.

Why Change Feels Hard

Change is one of the few constants in life, and yet it almost always unsettles us. Even when a change is welcome—such as retirement after years of work or a move to a new home—it can still stir up feelings of unease. Why? Because change disrupts the familiar patterns that make us feel safe.

From a psychological perspective, the human mind is wired to prefer stability. Routines, roles, and identities give us a sense of control, predictability, and belonging. When change arrives, that stability is shaken. A new chapter in life—whether expected or not—can feel like the ground has shifted beneath our feet. This is why transitions so often spark anxiety or resistance: We are losing something we knew, without yet knowing what will replace it.

On a biological level, change activates the stress response. The brain perceives uncertainty as a threat, triggering the fight, flight, or freeze response. Heart rate rises, muscles tense, and cortisol increases. It's useful against danger, but during life changes—such as retirement, illness, or children leaving home—it can cause ongoing anxiety when continuously activated and no actual threat is present.

Significant changes are deeply emotional because they affect our deepest attachments—to loved ones, routines, identities, and dreams. And resisting change in these areas only serves to deepen our suffering. It causes us to tighten up and dwell on what-if scenarios. It results in rumination that drains our energy and can manifest physically as headaches, tense shoulders, or fatigue.

Mindfulness helps us face these significant changes. If we pause to notice the stress in our bodies and how our minds create stories, we gain a deeper understanding. This understanding is the first step towards meeting significant transitions with clarity and balance.

Impermanence: Everything Arises and Passes

One of the most fundamental understandings we encounter in mindfulness practice is the concept of impermanence. At first, it sounds simple—even obvious. Of course, things change. We see it in the seasons, in our children growing, and in our own bodies as we age. But while our minds may understand this truth, our hearts often resist it. We want the good moments to last forever, and we want the hard ones to end as soon as possible.

Every breath we take is a reminder of this law of change. Inhaling, the body fills with life. Exhaling, it lets go. The breath never stays—it arises, completes itself, and passes. The same is true of our thoughts. One idea flickers into awareness, only to be replaced by another. Feelings, too, arrive unannounced: joy bubbling up in the chest, grief heavy in the throat, anger like heat in the face. Each one comes, lives for a moment, and dissolves.

And yet, our instinct is to cling. When joy arrives, we want to grasp it, hold it tight, make it stay. When sorrow comes, we fight it, push it down, or distract ourselves, hoping it will disappear. This pattern of clinging and resisting is a natural human impulse, but it's also what deepens our suffering. The joy we try to hold slips away anyway, leaving us disappointed. The pain we push away often grows stronger, demanding to be felt. What we resist not only persists but also weighs heavier on us.

Impermanence is not something to fear; it can become a source of freedom. Knowing that joy is fleeting shouldn't diminish it. It can make us more appreciative. We learn to fully inhabit those precious moments. Knowing that pain will not last forever helps us move through it, trusting that even the sharpest ache will eventually ease.

Mindfulness helps us rest in this truth. By paying close attention to our inner and outer worlds, we see impermanence everywhere. The sound of a bird comes and goes. The rise of tension in the shoulders builds and then releases. A thought insists on its importance, only to vanish into thin air. We start to notice that life is a stream of arising and passing, arising and passing. When we stop fighting that stream, we find a certain peace in simply being carried by it.

Clinging to what is passing only results in more stress and suffering. The more we grasp, the more we suffer. Impermanence teaches us to loosen our grip and to allow life to flow naturally.

This truth can feel unsettling at first, but with practice, it opens the heart. We realize that change is not only loss, but also possibility. Each ending makes way for a beginning. Each moment of letting go makes space for what comes next. By embracing impermanence, we align ourselves with the reality of life as it truly is—ever-changing, ever-unfolding. And in doing so, we discover that peace is not found in holding on, but in learning to let go.

Mindful Adaptability: Thriving Amidst Uncertainty

Building on previous mindfulness, the journey to mindful adaptability begins with acceptance, inviting us to acknowledge uncertainty and its associated thoughts and feelings, rather than resisting or trying to control them. Typically, during major life changes, people feel the need to take control, which often leads to overthinking, stress, and anxiety. For example, when a company restructures and your role is eliminated, the resistance can cause more fear. Accepting the change frees up mental space for new planning, networking, and exploring options that align with your values. Mindfulness helps us observe emotions without judgment, promoting non-reactivity—discussed in Chapter 8—leading to constructive actions instead of impulsive reactions.

Accepting the Present Moment

What is perhaps most misinterpreted about mindfulness is the notion that accepting the present moment is giving up or implies passivity. Acceptance is just the opposite. Mindful acceptance does not imply assenting to reality or being okay with pain, difficulty, or injustice. Acceptance is simply pausing long enough to allow us to see reality for what it is: We stop expending energy resisting what has already happened, and we respond from a clearer, steadier footing.

It in no way means allowing ourselves to be harmed or failing to act. Of course, we need to speak up and set boundaries when necessary. However, we often find ourselves in situations that are simply beyond our control. In those moments, acceptance becomes the gateway. In those moments, acceptance provides us space to breathe, access what is true, and act from a more grounded and balanced place.

When we meet the moment as it is, two things happen. First, we stop struggling with what can't be changed right now, which frees up our energy and softens our stress. Second, we make room for a thoughtful response—a choice guided not by fear or frustration, but by clarity, presence, and compassion. That's not passive. That's powerful.

If you're looking for a meditation that helps clarify and cultivate acceptance, consider my guided meditation, "Meditation on Acceptance: Meeting What Arises," available on Insight Timer.

Once we have accepted the present moment, we can move to curiosity. To practice curiosity, you have to move from "Why did this happen to me?" to "What can I learn right now?" or "What strength might I build in confronting this?" For example, when someone has a conflict with a partner, they often look for ways to blame their partner, or they might do the opposite and engage in endless self-criticism. Both are counterproductive to a wise solution. When we have the ability to shift to curiosity, we can ask meaningful questions about how to move forward in the relationship. Wise questions can help shift the dynamic from blame and defensiveness toward understanding, empathy, and problem-solving. The goal is not to "win" but to stay curious and open so both partners feel heard.

The most helpful questions are those that open space for understanding and connection. With mindful acceptance and the curiosity that follows, you might ask your partner how they are feeling and what hurts most, and explore what they need to feel supported. Stay curious by asking what you might be missing and whether you've understood them correctly. Reconnect by remembering what you both value in the relationship and how you can approach any issues together. Finally, look forward by asking what a good resolution would look like and what small steps each of you can take to resolve conflicts. These kinds of questions shift the focus from blame to empathy, clarity, and collaboration.

Mindfulness empowers us to change the way we treat ourselves, especially during challenging times. Many of us have a constant stream of self-criticism running in the background, so familiar and habitual that we barely notice it. We blame ourselves for feeling too much or not enough. We judge our reactions, replay our mistakes, and hold onto the idea that we should be handling life better. Mindfulness breaks that pattern gently. It makes us aware of those negative thoughts and encourages a different response—not with more judgment, but with the power of curiosity. Instead of asking, "What's wrong with me?" we start asking, "What's happening right now?" That small change, fueled by curiosity, creates room to breathe. And in that space, we begin to build strength.

Letting Go of "What Was" to Meet "What Is"

One of the most challenging aspects of navigating change is the yearning for how things used to be. Our memories of how things were can be bittersweet—on one hand, they remind us of what we loved; on the other, they make the present feel like a lesser version of life. We find ourselves looking back, as though if we stare hard enough, we could somehow reclaim "what was."

The trouble is that holding on to the past keeps us from inhabiting the present. When we cling to "what was," we resist "what is." That resistance manifests as tension in the body, heaviness in the heart, or a persistent whisper of dissatisfaction in the mind. It is not the change itself that causes the deepest suffering, but our refusal to accept that life has moved on.

Mindfulness offers us a different way. It teaches us to notice the ache of clinging without judgment, and to gently loosen our grip. Letting go does not mean forgetting the past or pretending it never mattered; it means embracing the present and moving forward. It means honoring what was, while recognizing that it no longer defines who we are now. It means allowing memories to live as memories—treasured, yes, but not prisons.

When we don't cling to "what was," we open the door to new possibilities. The present moment, even if unfamiliar or uncomfortable, has its own beauty and meaning. Meeting it fully requires courage, because it asks us to step into the unknown. But again and again, people who practice mindfulness discover that when they stop fighting the present, a peacefulness and stillness emerge.

In this sense, letting go is not a one-time act but a daily practice. Each breath, each change, each loss is another invitation to release our grip on yesterday and step into today. It is through this letting go that we discover freedom—not freedom from pain or loss, but freedom to live fully with what is here now.

Cognitive Reframing: Questioning Automatic Thoughts

When we are faced with change, it's not only the circumstances themselves that weigh on us—it's the thoughts we attach to them. Our minds generate automatic stories: "I can't handle this," "Things will never feel right again," or "They don't care about me." Such thoughts come so quickly and feel so convincing that we don't pause to ask whether they are true, even though much of our stress and anxiety comes not from the event itself, but from these unexamined beliefs.

Cognitive Behavioral Therapy (CBT) refers to this process as *cognitive reframing*. This refers to our ability to identify distorted or unhelpful thoughts and shift them toward more balanced and constructive perspectives. For example, instead of saying, "I will never adapt to retirement," we might reframe the thought as, "Adjusting to retirement is difficult, but I've adapted to many new situations before." This kind of questioning doesn't deny the difficulty of the transition—it simply opens space for hope and resilience alongside the challenge (Beck, 2011).

In a similar spirit, Byron Katie's "Four Questions," which we explored in an earlier chapter, offers another way of loosening the grip of stressful beliefs. Both CBT and Katie's approach rest on the same insight: Our minds are not always reliable narrators, and we do not have to believe every thought that comes to mind. By pausing to question our assumptions, we create the possibility of responding to change from a place of clarity rather than compulsion.

Reframing is not about replacing painful thoughts with artificially positive ones. It's about *not* believing that our thoughts tell the whole story.

Pivoting with Purpose

Pivoting with purpose means acting with intention, rather than reacting impulsively. Rather than acting out of fear or external pressure, mindful pivots encourage us to pause, ground ourselves, and choose the next steps based on our core values. Start by acknowledging uncomfortable feelings, such as anxiety or uncertainty, without letting them determine your actions. Next, ask clarifying questions, such as "What matters most in this moment?" and "Which option aligns with my goals and well-being?"

Use journal reflective—another tool from Chapter 8—to avoid hasty choices. For example, when considering whether to switch jobs, we could list our personal strengths and desired outcomes. Mindfully pivoting enables us to make choices that feel meaningful even when we don't know the outcome.

The pursuit of perfection is another mindset that often hinders smooth transitions. Perfectionism often manifests as an attempt to control and predict the future. We tend to overanalyze and criticize even minor mistakes. This mindset keeps us stuck and hinders our ability to move forward. With mindfulness, we can recognize perfectionistic thoughts and release them. We can respond with self-compassion instead of self-judgment.

Recognize progress, not just flawless execution. Embrace feedback as part of growth. This attitude shift increases flexibility, enabling you to adjust plans as conditions shift rather than clinging to a specific vision of success. Leaders navigating digital transformation admit they do not have all the answers. They invite diverse input, accept vulnerability, and tell authentic stories about setbacks and recoveries, rather than only celebrating wins. The willingness to experiment, fail, and adapt ultimately leads to solutions that perfectionism would never uncover.

Emotional resilience techniques, such as acceptance of the moment, non-reactivity, self-compassion, and open curiosity, anchor each stage of adaptability. Acceptance prevents additional stress from piling up, curiosity replaces fear with openness, intentional pivots offer direction based on our values, and embracing imperfection unlocks creativity and confidence. With this emotional foundation, we can now explore how to navigate the unpredictable nature of life's major transitions with flexibility and purpose.

Steadying Through Uncertainty

It is important that we learn ways to ground ourselves during significant transitions. I can vividly recall the first night that we lived in the city. In our country home, the nights were so still you could hear voices across the river miles away. In the city, I felt overwhelmed by the constant traffic and sirens. I remember feeling very restless and unsettled.

Mindfulness helped me stay present with that unease. Instead of pushing it away, I let myself feel the sadness of leaving behind what I loved. With time, I also began to notice the gifts of the city—new people, new opportunities, and even the grounding rhythm of paddling with a dragon boat team. Slowly, I realized that steadiness doesn't come from a place alone. It grows from how we meet what life brings—through presence, patience, and a willingness to keep showing up.

Practical steps also make a difference. Creating simple routines—a morning walk, shared meals, time for reading or hobbies—gave my days shape when everything felt unfamiliar. Routines don't have to be rigid. If something no longer works, you can swap it for something else. What matters is having a rhythm that steadies you when other parts of life feel unpredictable.

Trying new activities also helped me open up to this new chapter. Learning to play the trombone and dragon boating made me feel more grounded and fulfilled. Volunteering at Meals on Wheels and a homeless shelter provided a sense of purpose in connecting with others.

At the heart of all of this is purpose. Change can rattle and make us forget what matters most. The Personal Purpose Statement done previously can remind us of what is most important. Then we ask: Do my daily choices reflect this? When they do, even imperfectly, steadiness returns.

Mindful Decision-Making During Change

When we experience change, the road ahead is often very uncertain. There are many options, and decisions need to be made. Mindful decisions are different from simply responding out of habit based on anxiety or social pressure. Mindful decisions emerge from a consideration of our authentic selves, stem from our values, and are grounded in what is most important to us.

A mindful approach begins internally, by creating a space between stimulus and response. With mindful decision-making, we pause our hectic activity and bring our attention to what is arising in the moment, whether it be physical sensations, thoughts, or emotions. We acknowledge what's arising without rushing into action. This brief pause or space helps us transition from habitual reactivity to thoughtful engagement with the moment.

Reflection

I've realized that significant transitions feel unsettling because we feel we lack control. If we can let go of that control, a real peace and calm can settle in. Bringing mindfulness and intention to transitions allows me to feel less lost during these periods of uncertainty. Accepting what I cannot change and then becoming curious, rather than fearful, helps me find new strength each time life takes a different direction. Even small routines can feel stabilizing (while everything else feels shaky). These ways of relating to myself remind me that I can always choose how I respond, regardless of the challenges I face.

Adapting smoothly during transitions isn't about having everything figured out. It is quite the opposite. It's about listening to the subtle messages your body is sending and being able to listen to the still, quiet inner voice. It involves trusting the values that guide your life. If we can look at these transitions as an opportunity to pause and realign with what's most important, it can be a period of great joy and transformation.

Chapter 10:
Remembering to Remember: How to Make Mindfulness Stick

Some days, it seems easy to bring mindfulness into my life. But on other days, no matter how good my intentions are, I find myself in autopilot mode, bouncing from one task to the next, and forgetting to pay attention. The pace and demands of life can make it hard to remain present. I find myself questioning, "How can taking a moment to be present and mindful slip away so quickly when I know it benefits me?"

This chapter encourages a deep commitment to consistently practicing mindfulness. It offers clear strategies for integrating mindful attention into everyday routines and addresses common challenges that may arise along the way. If a formal meditation habit is your goal, this chapter offers pointers and methods for making it happen.

Remembering to Be Mindful

Conceptually, mindfulness is straightforward: pay attention to what is happening in the present moment, accept it, bring curiosity to it, understand it, and then proceed. But in practice, the hardest part is remembering. In my experience, the hardest part is the first step. If we don't remember to pay attention, we remain on autopilot and live out old habit patterns.

I struggled with this for decades at the early stages of my practice, and still do to some extent. I maintained a daily meditation practice, and I gained valuable insights along the way. But then I'd step into daily life, and suddenly get lost in thought, react on autopilot, and feel stressed. I knew the moment-to-moment awareness mattered, but I kept forgetting to actually do it.

So I came up with a solution: Post-it notes. I wrote two words on them: "Pay attention." And then I plastered them everywhere: on the dashboard of my car, the television, the bookshelf, my desk at work. At one point, there were so many Post-its that no matter where I looked, I'd see the reminder. Sometimes I'd roll my eyes at them, but most of the time, they did exactly what I needed: remind me to be aware. Those little yellow squares pulled me out of autopilot and back into the moment.

Not everyone needs a house and workplace full of Post-it notes. Then again, maybe we do. Either way, we all need reminders.

Here are some ways to help yourself remember to be mindful:

1. Use Visual Cues

Like my Post-its, visual cues can interrupt autopilot. You might write a word or phrase on a sticky note, wear a bracelet that catches your eye, or place a small object—like a stone or feather—where you'll see it often. Each time you notice it, come back to awareness of the moment. Research indicates that associating new behaviors with visible cues strengthens the habit loop (Duhigg, 2012).

2. Anchor Mindfulness to Daily Habits

Psychologists refer to this as "implementation intentions." It involves connecting mindfulness to an existing habit (Gollwitzer, 1999). For example: "If I brush my teeth, then I'll pause for one breath" or "If I walk on stairs, then I'll notice my body." These anchors turn ordinary routines into mindfulness cues. I know someone who set her kettle as her reminder. Every time the water boiled, she stood quietly, hands on the counter, breathing until it clicked off.

3. Set Digital Reminders

Phones and watches can serve as reminders. A soft chime at random times or a vibration on your wrist can be a cue to stop, notice your breath, and reconnect. One man I worked with set his computer calendar to display the words, "Where is your mind?" three times a day. He said it startled him at first, but over time, it became a friendly invitation to come back.

4. Create Small Rituals

Rituals help weave mindfulness into the rhythm of daily life. Take one conscious breath before getting out of bed, or end your day by recalling a single moment when you were truly present. Rituals provide both structure and meaning, turning mindfulness into something you naturally return to, like brushing your teeth or turning off the lights at night.

5. Practice Self-Compassion When You Forget

Forgetting is part of the practice. Every practitioner, regardless of their experience, can get lost in thought. What matters most is how we respond when we notice. Instead of scolding yourself, say: "Ah, I forgot. Now I'm back." Research on self-compassion indicates that treating ourselves with kindness enhances persistence in adopting healthy behaviors (Neff, 2011). Each time you remember is a success—a moment of mindfulness reclaimed.

The truth is, mindfulness doesn't require elaborate techniques. It requires remembering, again and again, to come back. Sometimes that remembering will come from a Post-it note, sometimes from the sound of a bird outside your window, sometimes from the ache in your back that says, "Pay attention, I'm here."

The more often we practice returning to the moment when we're lost in thought, the more natural it becomes. Perhaps this is why many mindfulness teachers refer to it as a mindfulness muscle. It's not unlike exercising a muscle in our body.

Making Mindfulness a Daily Habit

Building any lasting habit starts with understanding how habits form. Every habit involves cues, routines, and rewards (Becher, 2023). When you connect a new behavior to an existing routine, your brain can more easily recognize when and how to act. For example, I drink coffee every morning. I added a few minutes of mindful breathing to that routine. The familiar cue, either the smell or the act of brewing my coffee, reminds me to practice. Over time, this helped me integrate mindfulness into my mornings.

Identifying the routine activities that can be done mindfully is crucial for establishing new habits (Habit, 2024). For example, many people brush their teeth twice a day. Given this, you can make teeth brushing a core mindfulness practice. This would involve checking in with your posture as you brush, feeling the sensations in your feet, or noticing the motion of your arms.

One of my favorite anchors was walking up stairs. I set the intention to walk the stairs with presence, and if I found myself halfway and on autopilot, I would walk back and start over. It really worked for me. Another common anchor is checking your email after breakfast. Before diving into messages, pause and notice your breath, or take a moment to listen to the sounds around you. Eating meals also provides a consistent anchor. Before you start eating, pause to observe the colors and smells of your food. These everyday activities create convenient moments for practicing awareness, helping mindfulness become an integral part of your daily routine (Habit, 2024).

Mindfulness activities are simply the daily activities that serve as reminders to be present. Life offers dozens of potential anchors. Commuting to work can become a mindful transition. For example, while sitting in the car or on the bus, bring your attention to how the seat feels beneath you or the rhythm of your breath. If you take short breaks at work, designate the first sip of water from your bottle as a reminder to check in with your body's tension. Even walking through a doorway can be a subtle cue—a gentle reminder to pause and take a moment to notice your thoughts or surroundings. By intentionally pairing mindfulness with these ordinary actions, you train your mind to return to the present moment throughout the day (Becher, 2023; Habit, 2024).

Short mindfulness check-ins fit naturally into busy lives. These mini-practices can take as little as thirty seconds and still make a difference. When waiting at a red light, rather than letting impatience build, try focusing on three slow, deep breaths. Standing in line at a store gives you another opportunity; just plant your feet, relax your shoulders, and notice what you hear or see. Pause before picking up your phone; take that moment to ground yourself in the present moment.

Once mindfulness becomes a habit in these small moments, this will help you weather the typical and common obstacles you may face. Whether they are distractions, something comes up in your day that upsets you, or you simply aren't feeling motivated, keeping yourself grounded with these routines will help carry you through. A regular dedication to mindfulness practice will enhance your ability to stay present during times of challenge and ensure you feel prepared for whatever consequences may arise next.

Overcoming Common Roadblocks

We all face challenges in our mindfulness practice. Challenges such as distractions, discouragement, stale routines, and unrealistic expectations often appear on the path to sustaining mindfulness. Recognizing these roadblocks is the first step to moving past them.

Even seasoned practitioners find themselves pulled away by buzzing phones, worries about unfinished work, backaches, or sudden memories. Instead of fighting these distractions, acknowledge them gently.

It's normal to feel discouraged when life is busy or motivation wanes. There are times when you feel like you have practiced enough. Perhaps you skip practice days completely or sit down in a session and simply feel that nothing happened. That can lead you to think you are no good at it or to quit the practice altogether. It can be helpful to be aware of the way you speak to yourself about these experiences. Rather than being a critic of yourself in those moments, practice the response of being kind. You might say to yourself, "It's okay to have an off day."

Everybody gets derailed at times—even the mindfulness teacher or therapist with years of experience (Germer & Neff, 2019)! You may need to decide on some days to practice less, or simply take a step to practice mindfulness by taking a breath between activities. Each time you restart practice, remind yourself that consistency is built on kindness, not criticism or judgment. If it's helpful, consider designing a simple ritual to help you return to practice after a missed day, such as lighting a candle or writing down your intention.

Setting realistic expectations shields against disappointment. Mindfulness is not about staying perfectly focused or reaching enlightenment overnight. What is important in mindfulness is showing up for yourself, even if you are distracted half the time. For example, if your mind wanders ten times during a session but you bring it back each time, that is okay.

Progress often looks like gradually noticing more details about your own thinking or feeling less reactive in stressful situations, rather than sitting in perfect calm. For instance, you might find yourself responding patiently during an argument or remembering to pause before reacting at work. Celebrate each marker, no matter how small, because progress is cumulative (Dahl et al., 2020). Set goals you can achieve given your current stage of life. Adjust goals as needed so that mindfulness supports your overall well-being rather than becoming another source of pressure. Sustainable practice depends on flexibility and self-acceptance, not perfectionism.

Meditation Challenges

When I first began practicing meditation, I assumed stillness would come naturally if I just meditated long enough and breathed correctly. What I encountered instead was a flood of mental noise, unfinished conversations, anxious planning, old regrets, and new distractions. It felt like my brain had been waiting for this quiet moment just to throw a party. I remember sitting there thinking, "How is this helping?" What I didn't realize was that noticing the chaos wasn't a distraction from the practice; it was a part of it. It was the practice. Each time I caught myself lost in thought and gently returned to my breath, I was building the muscle of awareness. The point wasn't to eliminate thoughts but to stop letting them push me around.

Other challenges crept in, too. Drowsiness would sneak up during evening meditations. Sometimes, irritation showed up before I even sat down. And then there was the constant urge to check how much time had passed as if something more important might be waiting just outside the room. Over time, I learned to adjust. I began meditating when I felt more alert. I softened my expectations and shifted my posture when I noticed slouching into sleep. These weren't signs of failure. They were simply signals, reminding me to listen to my body and adjust with care rather than criticism.

What made the biggest difference was reflecting on my practice afterward. I'd pause for a few moments and ask: What came up today? Without judging, I would identify where I struggled with the practice. Because I realized that all obstacles are teachers rather than something to suppress, I could use them as learning tools. Perhaps they showed me where I clung to perfection, or perhaps where I could be more compassionate with myself. Bringing this kind reflection really helped me sustain a lifelong practice, especially through difficult times.

Looking to the Future: Embracing Growth and Wisdom

Building upon the mindfulness habits and resilience strategies developed in earlier chapters, we now turn to embracing growth and wisdom for the future. We've discussed mindful adaptability, reflective decision-making, and how some of the grounding practices we explored earlier can help us stay grounded during periods of transition. Building from that solid foundation, let's examine how to sustain and develop your mindful journey into the future.

Empowering Affirmations

Affirmations can be a great first step toward being mindful about growth, change, and transition in everyday life. They serve as gentle reminders of our capacity to grow, bounce back, and continue learning, regardless of the situation. Empowering affirmations can help us navigate uncertainty and self-doubt, allowing us to tap into our inner steadiness and energy to move forward. You can try using these affirmations in your morning or night routine by saying them aloud or by placing them somewhere to be seen and repeated daily (Carolan, 2025; Intelligent Change Mindful Affirmations, 2025):

- I honor my journey, knowing each day offers new opportunities for growth.

- I can bounce back and embrace each experience as an opportunity for learning.

- I embrace each transition as an opportunity for wisdom, renewal, and possibility.

- My strengths and insights offer me confidence and trust to navigate life's transitions.

- I choose to be curious and kind to myself as I grow and learn.

By routinely reflecting on these beliefs, you can cultivate emotional well-being and motivation. You can also personalize affirmations to align with your personal challenges and aspirations by altering them as you grow and evolve. You can also routinely reflect on your affirmations and use them to determine their ongoing relevance and support.

Letter to Your Future Self

As another way to deepen your mindful growth continuum, consider writing a letter to your future self. This reflective exercise will prompt you to clarify what you hope, intend, and dream of carrying forward. It helps you establish and reinforce your vision of where you want to be. It helps you clarify what matters most, bring your aspirations into focus, and plant seeds of intention that can support your growth. This was a core practice for me, and I repeated it several times during my first decade of mindfulness practice. At the last session of my MBSR course, I invited participants to write a letter to their future selves, and then, after a year had passed, I would mail the letters to them.

Step 1: Pause and Arrive

Find a quiet place. Sit comfortably, and let your attention settle into the present moment. Feel the support of the ground beneath you.

Ask yourself: "What do I need right now to be present?" Allow a sense of calm and openness before you begin writing.

Step 2: Imagine Your Future Self

Picture yourself six months, a year, or even five years from now. Imagine this version of you who has continued practicing mindfulness with sincerity. Notice:

- What qualities do they embody? Perhaps patience, steadiness, compassion, joy?

- How do they carry themselves in daily life?

- What challenges or transitions have they faced, and how have they met them?

Step 3: Begin Your Letter

Write as if you are speaking directly to your future self. You might begin with: *"Dear Future Me, I am writing to remind you of what you once longed for..."*

Here are some guiding prompts:

- Why did I begin practicing mindfulness? What do I hope it will bring to my life?

- What habits or qualities do I want to strengthen?

- How do I want to respond to difficulty and uncertainty?

- What gives my life meaning and purpose?

Write freely, without worrying about grammar, structure, or sounding wise. Let the words flow from your heart.

Step 4: Offer Encouragement

Include words of care and support for your future self. Imagine they are going through a difficult time. What encouragement would you give them? You might write:

- *"Even if you forget your practice, you can always begin again."*

- *"Remember the small joys: your breath, the trees, the kindness of others."*

- *"You are enough, just as you are."*

Step 5: Close with Intention

Conclude your letter with a blessing or a heartfelt aspiration. Something like:

- *"May you continue to grow in compassion."*

- *"May you meet each moment with steadiness and clarity."*

- *"May you always remember the freedom that is here, now."*

Step 6: Seal the Practice

When you're finished, fold your letter and place it in a safe location. You might choose a date to read it—perhaps six months or a year from now. Here is an example of a letter I once wrote:

Dear Future Me,

I hope this letter finds you well, living with presence, kindness, and balance. I am writing to remind you of what you once longed for, in case the busyness of life has blurred your vision.

You began this path of mindfulness to overcome anxiety and physical pain. Over time, this morphed into a desire to live more fully. You wanted to know yourself beyond the swirl of thoughts and the pull of old habits. You wanted to live from awareness, not from autopilot. You wanted to meet each moment—even the difficult ones—with acceptance and curiosity rather than fear or resistance.

I hope you have continued to nurture this practice. Remember the joy you felt in small pauses: the warmth of your breath in winter air, the taste of morning coffee, the moment of stillness before sleep, the awe of a sunset. These were not just fleeting pleasures; they were doorways into freedom.

If you are reading this in a season of doubt, know that the seeds you planted long ago are still alive. Each time you sat in silence, each time you met anger with patience or sadness with compassion, you watered those seeds. Growth isn't always visible, but it is always happening. Trust in that.

My wish for you is not that you are free of challenges—life will never be free of them—but that you carry them differently. That you meet them with steadiness, with the wisdom of knowing everything changes, and with the love that comes from remembering you are not separate from the rest of life.

And if you've strayed from the path for a while, don't worry. The present moment is always here, waiting for you to come home. One breath is enough to begin again.

With care,
Your Past Self

As you take time to reflect on the skills and awareness you have gained in this book, let acknowledgement and awareness take center stage. You have gathered a "toolbox" of practices that give you more confidence to move forward with the challenges you experience. Recognize what you have achieved for yourself, however minor it may feel. Mindfulness gives us the confidence to adapt to life's hurdles while remaining curious and courageous to face what lies ahead.

Remember, mindfulness is not a fixed destination. Instead, consider it an open-ended journey. Major transitions are simply a fresh start to a new chapter, which enables the potential for new discoveries and wisdom. Discover, learn, and make a difference by being open to opportunity. Over time, the seeds you plant through mindfulness practice will develop into deepening growth, resilience, and a deeper understanding of yourself. You continue to evolve with every choice made intentionally, and with every moment you practice presence.

Reflection

This chapter reminds me that mindfulness isn't a separate task on a to-do list—it becomes woven into the fabric of everyday life. The small choices are meaningful, whether it's taking a moment to breathe before picking up my phone, feeling my feet on the ground while waiting in line, or simply pausing for a "mindful" moment during a daily activity. These tiny moments are easy to overlook, but they help bring me back to the present, regardless of how busy or distracted I feel. If I can be kind to myself when I struggle to stay focused and celebrate those moments when I *do* remember, I shift into a mindset that is more open, compassionate, and accepting.

Meditation is very helpful for me. Spending up to 45 minutes in the morning connecting to life and letting it flow becomes a framework for my day. It supports creating those mindful moments. This is the art of what mindfulness is! It can be 30 minutes or ten minutes. The point is to start somewhere. You can do my Ten Minute Mindfulness Meditation on Insight Timer, and that's a good start!

After finishing my letters to my future self, I took a few moments to sit quietly and reflect. I notice what it felt like to put my hopes, values, and encouragement into words. Were there any themes that surprised me, or aspirations that felt especially alive? I reflected on whether my letter revealed areas of growth I want to nurture or qualities I already embody but sometimes overlook. I allowed myself to sit with whatever emotions arose, and I held them gently.

Over time, I have built mindfulness into my days, turning it into a steady habit. Part of this practice has been learning how to stay present even when life feels difficult or distracting, and part has been exploring how mindfulness can support me through various stages of life.

There will be challenges, but learning how to relate to distractions or setbacks with compassion and a flexible mindset means I can create the space to keep growing. I trust that the more I practice, the more I'll see how these mindful moments accumulate, making it easier to return to them and meet the future with greater calm and resilience. Each day is an opportunity to grow or an opportunity to reflect, deepen my understanding of myself, and embrace more of the world around me.

Conclusion

As I sit at the end of this journey with you, my heart is full of respect for the courage it takes to meet life's major transitions not with resignation, but with openness, acceptance, curiosity, and self-compassion. The book was designed to offer more than concepts. It was meant as an invitation to reclaim the present moment, with acceptance, no matter how uncertain or complex life may appear.

From the first attempts at mindful breathing to understanding what triggers your emotions and who you are now, this book has offered a range of practices rooted in mindfulness. Maybe journaling helped you see things more clearly, or maybe you surprised yourself by opening up to someone you trust. Each time you try, you take another step toward understanding yourself better. These chapters invited you to try, make mistakes, keep going, and learn a bit more about yourself along the way.

I hope this book provided the understanding that aging and the major transitions that come with it aren't a period of decline. It is a transitory gateway into purpose, growth, and enjoyment. Perhaps you have become comfortable with your feelings, or perhaps you embrace change as a wonderful part of a beautiful, unfinished process. Maybe you have been reframing your story and envisioning what could be written on the blank pages of your book as new stories of meaning and hope emerge. These epiphanies are so much more than intellectual insights. They are shifts in how you inhabit your life, marking the beginning of a powerful transition toward a more mindful and compassionate existence.

Facing life's transitions takes a deep openness and courage. We can feel alone or stuck. Showing up for yourself and doing the exercises and sitting with difficult emotions is a testament to your willingness to grow. If nothing else, I hope you recognize that this dedication is evidence of your readiness to thrive—not just endure but flourish and redefine what fulfillment means for you now.

Of course, the end of these pages is not the end of your journey. Mindfulness is a practice, not a destination, and there remains so much to explore. Perhaps you feel called to join a community of fellow travelers. Or you might be moved to connect with a meditation group, whether through an online forum or a local workshop. Or perhaps you wish to dive deeper into particular practices through digital tools, retreats, or further reading. Whatever path you choose, remember that everything you have learned here is adaptable. The practices can be tailored to fit your evolving needs and circumstances—return to them, reshape them, and let curiosity continue to guide you.

Connection has been a central theme throughout our exploration, and its importance only grows when shared. Your insights, struggles, and victories are not only valuable for your own healing—they can also inspire others. You might want to share your experience with family, friends, or a support group. All small actions ripple outward and create a web of support that helps you and those around you.

To help keep the momentum of being mindful in your everyday life, it's best to keep it simple and consistent. The easiest way to connect mindfulness to your existing activities is to tie it to a routine you already have in place. Perhaps in the morning while making coffee, or in the evening when you go for a walk. If meditation is for you, consider establishing a daily meditation habit by meditating at the same time each day with the help of a timer. When you are feeling adrift, you can revisit the journal prompts in this book and allow yourself to capture thoughts that may feel messy and unfinished.

Above all else, practice real-life mindfulness. It's okay to skip a day or two or find yourself back where you were before this experience. Every time you return to intentional awareness, it is a testament to your graciousness towards yourself, like another small stone on the foundation of resilience for the rest of your life.

I am filled with a deep sense of admiration for you in reading this book. I'm grateful for your openness in welcoming me into your life and such an intimate journey. Your willingness to be authentic and reflect honestly is heartwarming.

While I am one voice, this book exists because of the dozens of stories, questions, and hopes that people like you have shared—people committed to bringing some measure of compassion and renewal to the tide of change.

Let's think of this conclusion not as an ending, but as an invitation. I hope that you've learned that life's big transitions are not a narrowing of possibilities but rather a launchpad for discovery, creativity, and joy.

As you move forward, please take with you the same qualities that have served you throughout: curiosity to continue asking questions, compassion for yourself and others, and courage to lean into your next chapter with acceptance and an open heart. Your journey continues, bright with possibilities, and I am grateful and honored to be a part—even in a small way—of your unfolding journey.

If you found this book helpful, I'd be deeply grateful if you left an honest review. Your feedback helps others discover the book and supports the work of sharing these practices more widely.

References

Abu Rayhan. (2023, August 23). *Unleash your inner power: A comprehensive guide to self-improvement.* ResearchGate; RAYHANS. https://doi.org/10.13140/RG.2.2.34197.29920

Arlinghaus, K. R., & Johnston, C. A. (2018). The importance of creating habits and routines. *American Journal of Lifestyle Medicine, 12*(5), 451–453. https://doi.org/10.1177/1559827617745479

Bartlett, L., Buscot, M.-J., Bindoff, A., Chambers, R., & Hassed, C. (2021). Mindfulness is associated with lower stress and higher work engagement in a large sample of MOOC participants. *Frontiers in Psychology, 12,* 724126. https://doi.org/10.3389/fpsyg.2021.724126

Becher, N. (2023, April 5). *Master the habit loop: Change your life today.* Lemon8. https://www.lemon8-app.com/nicolebecher/7218648791275323910?region=us

Berk, L., Hotterbeekx, R., van Os, J., & van Boxtel, M. (2017). Mindfulness-based stress reduction in middle-aged and older adults with memory complaints: A mixed-methods study. *Aging & Mental Health, 23*(6), 643–650. https://doi.org/10.1080/13607863.2017.1347142

Black, D. S., & Slavich, G. M. (2016). Mindfulness meditation and the immune system: A systematic review of randomized controlled trials. *Annals of the New York Academy of Sciences, 1373*(1), 13–24. https://doi.org/10.1111/nyas.12998

Carolan, S. (2025, January 24). 125 powerful affirmations for growth mindset. *Loving Midlife*. https://lovingmidlife.co.uk/125-affirmations-for-growth-mindset/

Cramer, H., Lauche, R., Dobos, G., Langhorst, J., & Michalsen, A. (2019). Yoga for quality of life in older adults: A systematic review and meta-analysis. *Aging & Mental Health, 23*(9), 1093–1100. https://doi.org/10.1080/13607863.2018.1461196

Dragomir, K. (2024, November 9). Midlife crisis: Embracing maturity and wisdom. *Mindberg*. https://mindberg.org/midlife-crisis/

Farb, N. A., Segal, Z. V., & Anderson, A. K. (2013). Mindfulness meditation training alters cortical representations of interoceptive attention. *Social Cognitive and Affective Neuroscience, 8*(1), 15–26. https://doi.org/10.1093/scan/nss066

Fadeeva, A., Simmons, J., Thomas, L. B., Baker, K., & Ling, F. C. M. (2025). Retirement adjustment framework: Understanding the interplay between individual and contextual factors. *Journal of Prevention and Health Promotion*. https://doi.org/10.1177/26320770241279737

Gabzye. (2023, October 18). Harnessing the power of positive self-talk. *Lemon8*. https://www.lemon8-app.com/@gabzye/7291263584193462789?region=us

Gazerani, P. (2025). The neuroplastic brain: Current breakthroughs and emerging frontiers. *Brain Research*. https://doi.org/10.1016/j.brainres.2025.149643

Habit. (2024). Habit formation and behavior change: *The power of habits—How entrepreneurs can harness behavioral change for success*. FasterCapital. https://fastercapital.com/content/Habit-formation-and-behavior-change-The-Power-of-Habits--How-Entrepreneurs-Can-Harness-Behavioral-Change-for-Success.html

Hebb, D. O. (1949). *The organization of behavior: A neuropsychological theory*. Wiley.

Hill, L. A. (2022, February 14). Curiosity, not coding: 6 skills leaders need in the digital age. *Harvard Business School*. https://www.library.hbs.edu/working-knowledge/six-unexpected-traits-leaders-need-in-the-digital-era

Hoshaw, C. (2022, June 22). 32 mindfulness activities to find calm at any age. *Healthline*. https://www.healthline.com/health/mind-body/mindfulness-activities

How. (2024, March 14). *Personal purpose statement*. Simplish. https://simplish.co/blog/personal-purpose-statement

Huang, F., Hsu, A., Chao, Y., Shang, C. M., Tsai, J., & Wu, C. W. (2020). Mindfulness-based cognitive therapy on bereavement grief: Alterations of resting-state network connectivity associated with changes of anxiety and mindfulness. *Human Brain Mapping*, *41*(14), 3982–3995. https://doi.org/10.1002/hbm.25240

Huang, F.-Y., Hsu, A.-L., Hsu, L.-M., Tsai, J.-S., Huang, C.-M., Chao, Y.-P., Hwang, T.-J., & Wu, C. W. (2019). Mindfulness improves emotion regulation and executive control on bereaved individuals: An fMRI study. *Frontiers in Human Neuroscience*, *13*, 5. https://doi.org/10.3389/fnhum.2018.00541

Imbastoni, G. (2023, May 5). Create a personal vision statement and change your life. *BetterUp*. https://www.betterup.com/blog/create-a-personal-vision-statement

Infurna, F., Gerstorf, D., & Lachman, M. (2020). Midlife in the 2020s: Opportunities and challenges. *American Psychologist*, *75*(4), 486–498. https://doi.org/10.1037/amp0000591

Intelligent Change. (2025). *Mindful affirmations: 52 positive affirmation cards for women*. Intelligent Change.

Jamil, A., Gutlapalli, S. D., Ali, M., Oble, M. J. P., Sonia, S. N., George, S., Shahi, S. R., Ali, Z., Abaza, A., & Mohammed, L. (2023). Meditation and its mental and physical health benefits in 2023. *Cureus, 15*(6). https://doi.org/10.7759/cureus.40650

Jones, A. (2024, November 24). 10 mindfulness practices I recommend for inner peace. *Medium*. https://medium.com/@anna_luminous/10-simple-steps-to-start-your-mindfulness-journey-efd972360580

Katie, B., & Mitchell, S. (2002). *Loving what is: Four questions that can change your life*. Harmony Books.

Kemeny, M. E., Foltz, C., Cavanagh, J. F., Cullen, M., Giese-Davis, J., Jennings, P., ... Ekman, P. (2012). Contemplative/emotion training reduces negative emotional behavior and promotes prosocial responses. *Emotion, 12*(2), 338–350. https://doi.org/10.1037/a0026118

Keng, S. L., Smoski, M. J., & Robins, C. J. (2011). Effects of mindfulness on psychological health: A review of empiricalstudies. *Clinical Psychology Review, 31*(6), 1041–1056. https://doi.org/10.1016/j.cpr.2011.04.006

Kubicek, B., Korunka, C., Raymo, J. M., & Hoonakker, P. (2011). Psychological well-being in retirement: The effects of personal and gendered contextual resources. *Journal of Occupational Health Psychology, 16*(2), 230–246. https://doi.org/10.1037/a0022335

Kramer, G. (2007). *Insight dialogue: The interpersonal path to freedom*. Shambhala Publications.

Lang, D., Cone, N., Lally, M., Valentine-French, S., & Mather, R. (2022). Psychosocial development in middle adulthood. *Iowa State University Digital Press.* https://iastate.pressbooks.pub/

Mishchykha, L. P., Cherniavska, N., Kravchenko, V., Vityuk, N., Kulesha-Liubinets, M., & Khrushch, O. (2023). Application of mindfulness practices in work on stress reduction during the war. *Revista de Cercetare si Interventie Sociala, 81*(2), 39–58. https://doi.org/10.33788/rcis.81.2

Li, F., Harmer, P., Fitzgerald, K., Eckstrom, E., Stock, R., Galver, J., ... Batya, S. S. (2014). Tai Chi and postural stability in patients with Parkinson's disease. *New England Journal of Medicine, 366*(6), 511–519. https://doi.org/10.1056/NEJMoa1107911

Lindsay, E. K., Chin, B., Greco, C. M., Young, S., Brown, K. W., Wright, A. G. C., Smyth, J. M., Burkett, D., & Creswell, J. D. (2018). How mindfulness training promotes positive emotions: Dismantling acceptance skills training in two randomized controlled trials. *Journal of Personality and Social Psychology, 115*(6), 944–973. https://doi.org/10.1037/pspa0000134

Mayo Clinic. (2022, October 11). *Mindfulness exercises.* Mayo Clinic. https://www.mayoclinic.org/healthy-lifestyle/consumer-health/in-depth/mindfulness-exercises/art-20046356

McDaniel, M. A., & Einstein, G. O. (2000). Strategic and automatic processes in prospective memory retrieval: A multiprocess framework. *Applied Cognitive Psychology, 14*(7), S127–S144. https://doi.org/10.1002/acp.775

Miller, K. (2020, March 13). Building self-awareness: 16 activitie and tools for meaningful change. *PositivePsychology.com.* https://positivepsychology.com/building-self-awareness-activities/

Mitchell, B. A., & Teichman, S. (2024). Aging parents and the ties that bind: Intergenerational relationship quality among culturally diverse

Canadian families. *International Journal of Aging and Human Development, 98*(2), 151–170. https://doi.org/10.1177/00914150241240120

National Center for Complementary and Integrative Health. (2022). *Meditation and mindfulness: Effectiveness and safety*. NCCIH. https://www.nccih.nih.gov/health/meditation-and-mindfulness-effectiveness-and-safety

Debevoise, N. D. (2024, February 12). The power of a mindful morning routine. *Forbes*. https://www.forbes.com/sites/nelldebevoise/2024/01/30/the-power-of-a-mindful-morning-routine/

Neff, K. D. (2011). Self-compassion, self-esteem, and well-being. *Social and Personality Psychology Compass, 5*(1), 1–12. https://doi.org/10.1111/j.1751-9004.2010.00330.x

Nortje, A. (2020, July 8). 44 prompts, examples, and exercises: Journaling for mindfulness. *PositivePsychology.com*. https://positivepsychology.com/journaling-for-mindfulness/

Oh, V. K. S., Sarwar, A., & Pervez, N. (2022). The study of mindfulness as an intervening factor for enhanced psychological well-being in building the level of resilience. *Frontiers in Psychology, 13*, 1056834. https://doi.org/10.3389/fpsyg.2022.1056834

Ohlin, B. (2019, July 4). 7 ways to improve communication in relationships. *PositivePsychology.com*. https://positivepsychology.com/communication-in-relationships/

O'Bryan, A. (2021, December 4). How to perform body scan meditation: 3 best scripts. *PositivePsychology.com*. https://positivepsychology.com/body-scan-meditation/

Phillips, C. (2017). Lifestyle modulators of neuroplasticity: How physical activity, mental engagement, and diet promote cognitive health during aging. *Neural Plasticity*, *2017*, 3589271. https://doi.org/10.1155/2017/3589271

Positive Action Team. (2023, August 14). Empowering students with effective decision-making skills: A how-to guide. *Positive Action*. https://www.positiveaction.net/blog/empowering-students-with-effective-decision-making-skills

Reid, S. (2022, March 30). Midlife crisis: Signs, causes, and coping tips. *HelpGuide.org*. https://www.helpguide.org/aging/healthy-aging/midlife-crisis

Schuman-Olivier, Z., Trombka, M., Lovas, D. A., Brewer, J. A., Vago, D. R., Gawande, R., Dunne, J. P., Lazar, S. W., Loucks, E. B., & Fulwiler, C. (2020). Mindfulness and behavior change. *Harvard Review of Psychiatry*, *28*(6), 371–394. https://doi.org/10.1097/HRP.0000000000000277

Selva, J. (2018, April 23). Values clarification: How reflection on core values is used in CBT. *PositivePsychology.com*. https://positivepsychology.com/values-clarification/

Sutton, J. (2022, October 8). Inner child healing: 35 practical tools for growing beyond your past. *PositivePsychology.com*. https://positivepsychology.com/inner-child-healing/

Psychology Today. (2019, September 9). Swap out these anxious thoughts for better ones. *Psychology Today*. https://www.psychologytoday.com/us/blog/in-practice/201909/swap-out-these-anxious-thoughts-better-ones

Wayne, P. M., Manor, B., Novak, V., Costa, M. D., Hausdorff, J. M., Goldberger, A. L., ... Lipsitz, L. A. (2014). A systems biology approach to studying Tai Chi, physiological complexity, and healthy aging: Design and rationale of a pragmatic randomized controlled trial. *Contemporary Clinical Trials, 39*(1), 14–25. https://doi.org/10.1016/j.cct.2014.06.005

Wein, H. (2021, June). Mindfulness for your health. *NIH News in Health.* https://newsinhealth.nih.gov/2021/06/mindfulness-your-health

Wood, W., & Neal, D. T. (2007). A new look at habits and the habit-goal interface. *Psychological Review, 114*(4), 843–863. https://doi.org/10.1037/0033-295X.114.4.843

Wright, K. W. (2023, June 21). Emotional journaling: How to use journaling to process emotions. *Day One.* https://dayoneapp.com/blog/emotional-journaling/

Young, M. (2023, February 3). Body scan meditation for beginners: How and why to try it. *Cleveland Clinic.* https://health.clevelandclinic.org/body-scan-meditation

Inner Child Work. (2024, September 3). 80 inner child journal prompts for reparenting yourself. *Inner Child Work—Inner Child Therapy.* http://innerchildwork.co.uk/inner-child-journal-prompts/

www.ingramcontent.com/pod-product-compliance
Lightning Source LLC
Chambersburg PA
CBHW071208070526
44584CB00019B/2962